W9-BGB-043

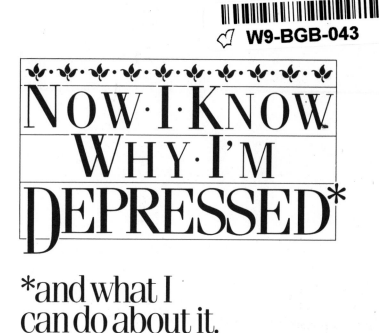

NOW·I·KNOW
WHY·I'M
DEPRESSED*

*and what I
can do about it.

H. NORMAN WRIGHT

HARVEST HOUSE PUBLISHERS
Eugene, Oregon 97402

Except where otherwise indicated, all Scripture quotations in this book are taken from the New American Standard Bible, Copyright © The Lockman Foundation 1960, 1962, 1963, 1968, 1971, 1972, 1973, 1975, 1977. Used by permission.

Verses marked AMP are taken from The Amplified Bible, Old Testament, Parts I and II, Copyright © 1964 and 1962 by Zondervan Publishing House, and from The Amplified New Testament, Copyright © The Lockman Foundation 1954, 1958. Used by permission.

Verses marked KJV are taken from the King James Version of the Bible.

Verses marked RSV are taken from the Revised Standard Version of the Bible, Copyright 1946, 1952, © 1971, 1973, by the National Council of the Churches of Christ in the U.S.A. Used by permission.

Verses marked TLB are taken from The Living Bible, Copyright 1971 by Tyndale House Publishers, Wheaton, Illinois. Used by permission.

NOW I KNOW WHY I'M DEPRESSED

Copyright © 1984 by Harvest House Publishers
Eugene, Oregon 97402

Library of Congress Catalog Card Number 84-81216
ISBN 0-89081-423-6

Printed in the United States of America.

Contents

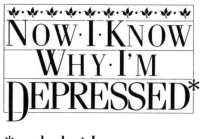

NOW·I·KNOW WHY·I'M DEPRESSED*

*and what I
can do about it.

1

What Is Depression?

For many years you have been a fairly happy and easygoing person. You have been conscientious at work and involved with your family. You have had few physical complaints. But lately something has changed. You find yourself acting differently. People who know you say, "You're just not yourself anymore." What's going on?

You find it difficult to get out of bed in the morning; if you have responsibilities for other family members you let them shift for themselves. You're becoming indecisive and even forgetful. Your ability to concentrate seems to have fled. You don't feel like laughing, food seems to have lost its taste, and sex has lost its appeal. You seem to be withdrawing into a shell, not wanting to be bothered by family or friends. And you don't care to talk on the phone or attend the social gatherings you used to enjoy. You're starting to sever all contact with other people.

Perhaps you have difficulty falling asleep at night, or perhaps you awaken in the middle of the night and thrash about until dawn, disturbed by negative and gloomy thoughts. You would like to sleep 16 hours a day or take frequent naps. But no matter how much you sleep, you still feel exhausted.

Your thoughts are filled with hopelessness. There doesn't seem to be any way out of your circumstances. You feel that no ones cares about you, and you don't particularly care for yourself either. Any positive feelings about yourself have long since gone. You feel as though there were a dark thundercloud hanging above your head following you wherever you go.

Physically you may note some changes. You have a number of new vague pains or aches; you may be convinced that you have some serious disease.

If you are experiencing the symptoms just described, or have ever experienced them, then you know what it is like to be depressed. If you have never experienced depression to any degree (which would be rare indeed), you need to know that depression is painful for the one who experiences it and at times for the person's loved ones as well.

Depression has been called "the common cold of the mind." Mental health experts conservatively estimate that one in every ten people in our country suffers from this affliction. This is a conservative estimate because in its milder forms depression often goes unnoticed and undetected.

Depression affects the whole person. Even though we may not be aware of it, when we are depressed all areas of our life are affected. There are biological-medical aspects, emotional-psychological aspects, and significant spiritual aspects. Depression affects our roles and relationships—

our work, play, friendships, marriage, and family, as well as our involvement with church and community.

What causes depression? How widespread is it? How normal is it to be depressed? Who gets depressed? Are some people depression-prone? What should you do when you get depressed? What can you do when your spouse or child begins to get depressed? Do all depressed persons think about suicide? Is it a sin to be depressed?

In this book we will attempt to provide some answers.

The Common Symptom

Emotional depression is probably the most common symptom in our country today. Some observers have noted that if the fifties were the age of anxiety, then the seventies were the age of melancholy or depression. The number of cases of depression has risen to the level of a national epidemic. One out of every eight Americans can be expected to require treatment for depression at some time during his lifetime. In any one year it is estimated that between 4 and 8 million people are depressed to the extent that they cannot effectively function at their jobs or must seek some kind of treatment.

Is depression the cause for the higher rates of suicide in America today? Well, not all depressed people get to the point where they are suicidal. Depression can cover a very broad spectrum, ranging from brief periods of moodiness to long-lasting, chronic periods of total despair. Deep, long-lasting, chronic depression may very well result in suicide. Suicide now ranks as the fifth-largest killer in the 15-to-55 age group. Dr. Bertram Brown, director of the National Institute of Mental Health, has stated that of those people who have clearly committed suicide, over 80 percent of them were found to have been definitely depressed. One of the most common things that occurs prior to suicide is depression.[1]

At some time in our lives depression affects each of us. No one is immune, not even the Christian. Some people will experience depression on a shallow level while others dive to the depths of despondency. The psalmist reflected these deep feelings of sorrow when he wrote:

> The Lord is close to those who are of a broken heart, and saves such as are crushed with sorrow for sin and are humbly and thoroughly penitent (Psalm 34:18 AMP). O Lord, the God of my salvation, I have cried to You for help by day; at night I am in Your presence. Let my prayer come before You and enter into Your presence; incline Your ear to my cry! For I am full of troubles, and my life draws near to the realm of the dead. I am counted among those who go down into the pit; I am as a man who has no help or strength—a mere shadow; cast away among the dead, like the slain that lie in a grave, whom You remember no more, and they are cut off from Your hand (Psalm 88:1-5 AMP).

Writers in ancient times described depression as melancholia. The first clinical description of melancholia was made by Hippocrates in the fourth century B.C. He also referred to mood swings similar to mania and depression (Jelliffe, 1921).

Aretaeus, a physician living in the second century A.D., described the melancholic patient as "sad, dismayed, sleepless.... They become thin by their agitation and loss of refreshing sleep.... At a more advanced state, they complain of a thousand futilities and desire death."

Plutarch, in the second century A.D., presented a particularly vivid and detailed account of melancholia:

> He looks on himself as a man whom the gods hate and pursue with their anger. A far worse lot is before him; he dares not employ any means of averting or of remedying the evil, lest he be found fighting against the gods. The physician, the consoling friend, is driven away. "Leave me," says the wretched man, "me, the impious, the accursed, hated of the gods, to suffer my punishment." He sits out of doors, wrapped in sackcloth or in filthy rags. Ever and anon he rolls himself, naked, in the dirt confessing about this and that sin. He has eaten or drunk something wrong. He has gone some way or other which the Divine Being did not approve of. The festivals in honor of the gods give no pleasure to him but fill him rather with fear or a fright (Quoted by Zilboorg, 1941).[2]

Walter Trobisch, a Christian counselor, notes that the word for depression in German is *schwermut*. *Schwer* can mean "heavy" as well as "difficult." *Mut* is the word for "courage." So the word *schwermut* contains a positive message: It means the courage to be heavyhearted, the courage to live with what is difficult.

Strange as it may seem, courage is a part of depression. There is even such a thing as the gift of depression—a gift which enables us to be "heavy," to live with what is difficult. Once I heard an experienced psychiatrist say, "All people of worth and value have depressions." Indeed, superficial people seldom have depressions. It requires a certain inner substance and depth of mind to be depressed.

Suicide can be an indication of a person's inability to be depressed. For the person lacking depth in his personality it may be much easier for him to cut the thread of life. The philosopher Landsberg's comment in this regard becomes increasingly meaningful the more one contemplates it: "Often a man kills himself because he is unable to despair and endure depression." The suicidal person lacks the courage to be depressed. Martin Luther went so far as to encourage "believing in the blessing of depression."

As devastating as depressive illness can be, it can also be turned to good account. "Depression is a sign that something is not right in your life," says Yale's Dr. Murna Weissman. "If you pay attention to that sign and use the experience constructively to make changes, it can be a strengthening and sobering experience. I wouldn't prescribe it, but it doesn't necessarily have to be detrimental and destructive."

For Percy Knauth, author of *A Session in Hell,* the experience of depression was a positive one. "I had more depth, more compassion—about myself and toward my fellow man. I had learned a great deal about the human psyche and the strange ways in which it works. I felt better equipped to meet the stresses of living in an unsettled world, and better able to understand the motivations of others around me.

"Viewed in this sense, the depression I suffered through was an enriching and rewarding life event."[3]

In many cases depression is a healthy response to what is taking place in a person's life. Being depressed is not a sin. It is a normal reaction to what is happening to us psychologically and physically. Depression is a scream, a message, telling us that we have neglected some area of our lives. We must listen to the depression, for it is telling us something we need to know. It is a signal that something in our lives is not right; we must respond to the message.

"Unfortunately, within society in general and particularly within the Christian community, depression is stigmatized as sinful and indicative of weakness and spiritual inadequacy. Nevertheless, Charles Spurgeon, the great nineteenth-century preacher, saw depression as far from sinful, although painful.

"Spurgeon describes some of the times when depression most often occurs for all of us:

> The times most favorable to fits of depression, so far as I have experienced, may be summed up in a brief catalogue.
>
> First, among them I mention *the hour of great success.* When at last a long-cherished desire is fulfilled, when God has been glorified greatly by our means, a great triumph achieved, then we are apt to faint. . . .
>
> *Before any great achievement,* some measure of the same depression is very usual. Surveying the difficulties before us, our hearts sink within us. . . . This depression comes over me whenever the Lord is preparing a larger blessing for my ministry. . . .
>
> *In the midst of a long stretch of unbroken labour,* the same affliction may be looked for. The bow cannot be always bent without fear of breaking. Repose is as needful to the mind as sleep to the body. . . .
>
> *This evil will also come upon us, we know not why,* and then it is all the more difficult to drive it away. Causeless depression is not to be reasoned with. . . . If those who laugh at such melancholy did but feel the grief of it for one hour, their laughter would be sobered into compassion. . . .
>
> If it be inquired why the valley of the shadow of death must so often be traversed by the servants of King Jesus, the answer is not far to find.

All this is promotive of the Lord's mode of work-ing, which is summed up in these words: "Not by might nor by power, but my Spirit, saith the Lord . . . ."

Heaven shall be all the fuller of bliss because we have been filled with anguish here below, and earth shall be better tilled because of our train-ing in the school of adversity.

"Certainly Spurgeon's words speak of anything but stigma. Rather they encourage depressed persons to know they may be molded into special instruments for God's service. Depression may not be something any of us would seek, but it is an emotion that can be used rather than wasted. Of all things in this world worse than suf-fering, wasted suffering is certainly high on the list."[4]

Depression has both spiritual and emotional elements to it as its darkness gradually draws a veil over our life. Joy and peace are replaced by unhappiness and discontentment. Instead of the experience of being filled with the Spirit, there is barrenness. Faith and hope give way to doubt and despair. We do not feel loved and forgiven. If anything, we feel unworthy, guilty, and aban-doned. We feel as though we have been left alone to tromp through the darkness in isolation. And we doubt and doubt and doubt. Certainty is no longer a part of our life. We have no assurance of God's loving care, and we feel like an orphan.

It is so important to remember that, especially

when we are depressed, we cannot depend upon good and bubbly feelings to confirm our faith. When we are unable to feel God's presence, and we feel abandoned, this is the time to hold firmly to the facts of the Word of God that tell us He is there and we are not alone. If we believe that God is not around because we do not feel Him, then because we do not feel Him, we will not reach out in an act of faith to rely upon Him. But the outreached arms of Jesus are always there. Sometimes we may need to ask a friend to loan us his faith so that we can reach out and accept God's help.

Richard Berg tells the story of a small child who is caught on the second floor of a burning house. He goes to the window of the bedroom, alone and frightened, and cries out for help. His father looks up and calls to him, "Jump, son—I'll catch you!" But the child responds, "But I can't see you, Daddy, I can't see you! I'll fall!" The child is so frightened that he will not move. The smoke has clouded his vision, and he cannot see his father below him. "But, son, I can see *you!* Jump and I will catch you."

Sometimes we are like the frightened child. We cannot feel God and therefore will not take that leap of faith. But even when we feel that His presence has been extinguished, He is there and waiting. We must let Him walk with us in our depression and lead us out of it.

Preserve me, O God, for I take refuge in Thee

(Psalm 16:1). I have set the Lord continually before me; because He is at my right hand, I will not be shaken (Psalm 16:8). For Thou dost light my lamp; the Lord my God illumines my darkness (Psalm 18:28). The Lord is my light and my salvation; whom shall I fear? The Lord is the defense of my life; whom shall I dread? (Psalm 27:1). Hear, O Lord, when I cry with my voice, and be gracious to me and answer me (Psalm 27:7). God is our refuge and strength, a very present help in trouble (Psalm 46:1). Be gracious to me, O God, according to Thy lovingkindness; according to the greatness of Thy compassion blot out my transgressions (Psalm 51:1). Create in me a clean heart, O God, and renew a steadfast spirit within me (Psalm 51:10). Cast your burden upon the Lord, and He will sustain you; He will never allow the righteous to be shaken (Psalm 55:22). My soul waits in silence for God only; from Him is my salvation (Psalm 62:1).

2

Who Gets Depressed?

Depression affects everyone—men and women, people of all ages, the rich and the poor. Just because a person is successful does not mean that he is protected from the possibility of depression. Nor are certain types of people more prone to depression than others. Artists, movie stars, politicians, people who are in the public spotlight, creative and sensitive people, high achievers, and celebrities are no more depression-prone than anyone else. These people are just more visible than others; if they become depressed, the whole world seems to know about it.

The one type of person who may be a bit more vulnerable to depression than most is the one who has experienced nothing but success from early childhood. If he has never tasted of defeat, he may crumble at the first setback.

Are women more prone to depression than men? Women are treated for depression two or three times as often as men. But this evidence is based upon visits to clinics; and clinics are mostly open in the daytime, when men are at work. Also, our society traditionally allows women to admit weaknesses or problems and to seek help, but insists that men maintain stability and put up a brave front. Unfortunately, males in our culture have been taught not to admit weakness and not to reveal their inner feelings. It is interesting to note that male alcoholics outnumber female alcoholics significantly; and the rate for successful suicides is three times higher for men than for women. Men perhaps deal with their depression differently than women do.

Ninety-five percent of even the severely depressed can be totally cured if the condition is identified early enough. And the everyday, minor depressive episodes can certainly be overcome. But it is important to heed the early-warning signs of depression and act immediately.

Many people ask, "How long does a bout of real depression actually last?" Dr. Aron Beck of the University of Pennsylvania says an episode of depression usually "bottoms out" within three weeks. After that the person is usually diagnosed and help is sought, either from family members or a physician or a counselor. If help is not received, the depression could become worse than it has to. Dr. Floyd Estess of Stanford University Medical School Psychiatry Clinic estimates that a person with one untreated attack of depression runs a 50-50 risk of a second attack within three years.[5]

What Depression Is Like

Let's examine in detail what it is like to be depressed. Here are ten of the most common characteristics of depression.

1. The person experiences a general feeling

of hopelessness, despair, sadness, apathy, and gloom. Richard Berg describes it as a "spiritual sadness."

> Sadness is a wound deep within the spiritual self-concept. It often produces a considerable suffering for the depressed person and may be viewed as a "tree that thrives in darkness." The twin roots of this tree—(1) the belief that one is unloved, with the perplexing inability to forgive (resentment), and (2) the belief that one is unlovable, with resistance to accepting forgiveness (perfectionism)—distort one's perception of the present and dim one's expectations for the future. This "tree" of darkness cannot flourish in the light which God's unconditional and healing love brings. The Lord longs to heal spiritual sadness by leading us out of darkness: he brings glad tidings to the lowly, heals the broken-hearted, proclaims liberty to captives and release to those who are prisoners (Isaiah 61:1).
>
> In fact, Jesus said of himself, "I am the light of the world. No follower of mine shall wander in the dark; he shall have the light of life" (John 8:12).
>
> The psalmist exults in God's healing, loving presence: "You indeed, O Lord, give light to my lamp; O my God, you brighten the darkness about me" (Psalm 18:28).[6]

The wound of sadness is tied to guilt, emptiness, and doubt. There is guilt over one's sense of imperfection. It is no surprise that many people who struggle with depression are perfectionists. They set standards so high that they are easy targets for failure. Because of the apparent failures they feel a weight or burden.

Jesus responds to all of us who experience guilt: "And behold, they were bringing to Him a paralytic, lying on a bed; and Jesus seeing their faith said to the paralytic, 'Take courage, son; your sins are forgiven' " (Matthew 9:2 AMP). "Come to Me, all who are weary and heavy-laden, and I will give you rest. Take My yoke upon you, and learn from Me, for I am gentle and humble in heart; and you shall find rest for your souls. For My yoke is easy, and My load is light" (Matthew 11:28-30).

There is a sense of emptiness. The depressed person has no hope and believes he is unloved. He feels he has no friends or people who care about him. The psalmist expressed such feelings when he wrote, "O Lord, the God of my salvation, I have cried out by day and in the night before Thee. . . . For my soul has had enough troubles, and my life has drawn near to Sheol. I am reckoned among those who go down to the pit; I have become like a man without strength, forsaken among the dead, like the slain who lie in the grave, whom Thou dost remember no more, and they are cut off from Thy hand. . . . I was afflicted and about to die from my youth on; I suffer Thy terrors; I am overcome" (Psalm 88:1,3-5,15).

Jesus responds to us by saying, "The thief comes only to steal, and kill, and destroy; I came that they might have life, and might have it abundantly" (John 10:10). "These things I have spoken to you that My joy may be in you, and that your joy may be made full" (John 15:11).

The depressed person's doubts about himself and whether other people love him soon develop into resentment. If he does not express and deal with this resentment, it can feed his depression. What does the Word of God say to us?

> For God so loved the world that He gave His only begotten Son, that whoever believes in Him should not perish, but have eternal life (John 3:16). What do you think? If any man has a hundred sheep, and one of them has gone astray, does he not leave the ninety-nine on the mountain and go and search for the one that is straying? And if it turns out that he finds it, truly I say to you, he rejoices over it more than over the ninety-nine which have not gone astray. Thus it is not the will of your Father who is in heaven that one of these little ones perish (Matthew 18:12-14). I am the good shepherd. The good shepherd lays down His life for the sheep (John 10:11).[7]

2. When a person is depressed he loses perspective. The way he views his life, his job, and his family is colored. As one man put it:

> There's a real difference between being unhappy and being depressed. When my wife and I have an occasional argument, I'm unhappy about it. I don't like it. But it's part of living. We make up in a fairly short time. I may be concerned over

it, but I can sleep all right, and I still feel in good spirits. But when I'm depressed, that's a different matter. It hurts all over; it's almost something physical. I can't get to sleep at night, and I can't sleep through the night. Even though there are still times when I'm in pretty good spirits, the mood comes over me nearly every day. It colors the way I look at everything. If my wife and I have a fight our marriage seems hopeless. If I have a business problem, which I would normally react to with some tension and frustration but which I deal with promptly and appropriately, I feel as though I'm a lousy businessman and I battle with the problems of self-confidence instead of dealing with the issues in front of me.[8]

Depression distorts our perception of life. Each of us perceives life from our backlog of experiences. Our memories are always with us, and they influence the way we perceive life, giving us a sense of expectancy. Our perceptions happen automatically and we believe that what we perceive is the real world.

Richard F. Berg describes our ability to perceive as similar to a camera. Photographers can alter the image of reality through the use of various lenses or filters. Thus a camera might not provide an accurate view of the world. A wide-angle lens gives a much wider panorama but the objects appear more distant and smaller. A tele-photo lens has a narrower and more selective view of life. It can focus on a beautiful flower, but in so doing it shuts out the rest of the garden.

Happy and smiling people seen through a fish-eye lens instead of a normal one appear distorted and unreal.

Filters can blur reality, break up images into pieces, bring darkness into a lighted scene, or even create a mist. Thus a photographic view of the world can be distorted. When we are depressed our perception of the world becomes distorted. Depression becomes like a set of camera filters which focus upon the darker portions of life and take away the warmth, action, and joy from a scene. A photographer is aware of the distortion that he is creating as he switches lenses. The depressed person, however, is not very aware of the distortion that he is creating as he switches lenses. When we are depressed we are partially blind without knowing it. And the greater the intensity of our depression, the greater the distortion.

What do we distort? We distort life itself. It loses its excitement and purpose. We distort the image of God. We see Him as far away and uncaring. There appears to be a tremendous gulf or wall separating us from God. And we also distort our own view of ourselves. Our worth, value, and abilities have vanished.

Part of the journey for the depressed person is to change the distorted lens of his mind to a realistic one. Usually we need help from other people to do that. If we are depressed we need to ask for help. If we know someone who is depressed, we need to minister to that person as the friends of the blind man in the Gospel of Mark ministered to him.

> And they came to Bethsaida. And they brought a blind man to Him, and entreated Him to touch him. And taking the blind man by the hand, He brought him out of the village; and after spitting on his eyes, and laying His hands upon him, He asked him, "Do you see anything?" And he looked up and said, "I see men, for I am seeing them like trees, walking about." Then again He laid His hands upon his eyes; and he looked intently and was restored, and began to see everything clearly (Mark 8:22-25).

The friends took action for the blind man. But the blind man trusted his friends and allowed them to lead him to Jesus. Patiently we need to lead our depressed friends to Jesus. And if we are depressed ourselves, we must allow others to lead us to the One who can open our eyes. In our blindness we need a guide. Read over and over the hopeful words from the Book of Isaiah: "I will lead the blind on their journey; by paths unknown I will guide them. I will turn darkness into light before them, and make crooked ways straight. These things I do for them, and I will not forsake them" (Isaiah 42:16)[9]

3. The depressed person experiences changes in physical activities—eating, sleeping, sex. Sexual interest wanes, and some men find that they cannot perform. This reinforces their feelings of worthlessness. A lessening of sexual interest should always raise the question of whether the

person is suffering from depression. Some people lose interest in food, whereas others attempt to set a world record at gorging themselves. Some sleep constantly, while others cannot sleep at all.

4. There is a general loss of self-esteem. The person feels less and less positive about himself, and questions his own personal value. Self-confidence is at an all-time low.

5. The depressed person withdraws from other people because of a groundless fear of being rejected. Unfortunately, the depressed person's behavior may actually produce some rejection from others. The depressed person cancels favorite activities, fails to return phone calls, and seeks ways to avoid talking with or seeing others.

6. There is a desire to escape from problems and even from life itself. Thoughts of leaving home or running away, as well as avoiding other people, are common. Suicidal thoughts enter because of the feeling that life is hopeless and worthless.

7. A depressed person is oversensitive to what other people say and do. He may misinterpret actions and comments in a negative vein and become irritable because of these mistaken perceptions. Often the person cries easily because of wrong interpretations.

8. The person has difficulty in handling most of his feelings, especially anger. Anger can be misdirected toward oneself and toward others. The anger at oneself is based upon feelings of

worthlessness and a lack of knowing how to deal with the situation. Often this anger is directed outward toward others.

9. Guilt is another characteristic of depression. The basis for the guilt may be real or imagined. Frequently, guilt feelings arise because the depressed person assumes that he is somehow in the wrong or that he is responsible for making other people miserable because of his depression.

10. Often depression leads to a state of dependence upon other people. This reinforces the person's feelings of helplessness, and he becomes angry at his own helplessness.

It is important to remember that once a person starts becoming depressed, he usually behaves in a way that reinforces the depression. Read back over the previous description of depression and you will begin to see how this happens.

One of the most common questions that Christians ask about depression concerns sin. "Is depression a sin? Is it a sin for a Christian to be depressed?" In and of itself depression is not sin. Depression is sometimes a consequence of sin, but not always. It can be a symptom of sin and thus serve as a warning to us. A husband who beats his wife or is unfaithful may experience both guilt and depression as a result of his behavior. He is being warned, and his depression is the consequence of what he is doing.

Many people are surprised to read the account of Jesus' depression in the Garden of Gethsemane. Jesus was a perfect man and free from all sin, yet complete in His humanity and tempted as we are. Look at the account in Matthew 26:36-38:

> Then Jesus went with them to a place called Gethsemane, and He told His disciples, "Sit down here while I go over yonder and pray." And taking with Him Peter and the two sons of Zebedee, He began to show grief and distress of mind and was deeply depressed. Then He said to them, "My soul is very sad and deeply grieved, so that I am almost dying of sorrow. Stay here and keep awake and watch with Me" (AMP).

Jesus knew what was about to happen to Him, and it caused Him to be depressed. He did not feel guilty over being depressed, and neither should we. But this is sometimes difficult because our depression creates a distortion of life. It also intensifies any guilt feelings that we have. So guilt over depression leads to more depression.

Dr. Archibald Hart describes the positive aspect of depression.

> Depression is a symptom which warns us that we're getting into deep water. It is, I believe, designed by God as an emotional reaction to slow us down, to remove us from the race, to pull us back so we can take stock. I would even say that it is designed to drive us back to God in terms of trust and resources. It is a protective device which removes us from further stress and gives us time to recover.[10]

This question really ties into the larger question of why God allows us to be sick or to sin. As humans, we have been designed to experience emotion, not just joy, but sadness as well. Perhaps the dark side of our emotions is to drive us to God. If we were happy all the time, maybe we wouldn't feel we needed God. With depression there is certainly a positive side. God has created us with the ability to experience depression for a very good reason, I believe.

Depression is like pain. While pain is inconvenient, it is a warning system, essential for our survival. We wouldn't ask, "Why does God allow me to experience pain?" If I felt no pain, I'd be killed the first day I walked out my front door. God also has created me with the ability to experience depression so that I can have a very important warning system to tell me when things are wrong. But He doesn't allow me to be depressed in the sense of sending it my way as a form of punishment. He has taken all my punishment on the Cross. But He has given me a wonderful gift in depression which I should be able to use as an important warning system. If we can make that distinction, I think we will avoid reacting in an unhealthy way to the depression itself. This will only intensify it.[11]

Becoming depressed is a common psychobiological response to stress. We cope with the stresses of life on both a physical and a psychological level. Every thought and feeling can produce a change in the chemistry of our nervous system. As we look at the numerous causes for depression we see the extent of this relationship.

Dr. Frederick Flach has suggested that most people in our society are very well defended against knowing themselves. Any event or change in a person's life that forces him to break any of his defenses can be painful. To experience acute depression can be an opportunity for a person to learn more about himself and also to become more whole than he was before.

Dr. Theodore Rubin has stated that being depressed is a signal that a change is needed. This can be one of the most constructive times in a person's life—if he responds to the signals. Depression can clear the air and help a person rid himself of years of accumulated anger and hurt. By doing this the depressed person can move toward feeling warmth and love, and can reevaluate his expectations of life, of himself, and of other people.[12]

Unfortunately, we are often threatened by our own depression; we wonder whether we have been sinning or have failed the Lord in some manner. We are also threatened by depression in another believer, especially if it is our own spouse.

It is difficult to know how to respond to the depressed person. Instead of responding to depression as a signal and finding the cause, we find it tempting to tell the person, "Snap out of it," or, "A true Christian doesn't get depressed," or, "Don't you know that being depressed is a sin?" If you were depressed and someone said that to you, how would you feel? Would you get better or would you go deeper into your despondency?

Unfortunately, many of us have heard pastors preach that being depressed is a sin in and of itself. Every time I hear that I cringe. I hurt for the people in the congregation who may be depressed. I wonder what that kind of message does to them.

Often when counseling a person experiencing depression I will ask, "Is there any way that you could thank God for being depressed?" The response is usually a puzzled look. Depression hurts. What could I possibly mean by thanking God for it? I might say, "Perhaps it is a signal that some other area of your life is crying out for recognition and help. If you weren't depressed you could be in even worse shape!"

We need to see depression as a message to which we need to respond as soon as possible. As we look at the many causes for depression we will see why this is true. We will also note several people in the Scriptures who experienced depression, and we will explore what it meant in their lives.

What happens to us spiritually when depression occurs? Are there any predictable symptoms or tendencies? Two extremes usually occur. The most common is to withdraw from God. We tend not to pray or read the Scriptures as we once did. Why? Possibly because we feel that God has either rejected or abandoned us. Because guilt is a part of depression, we tend to feel that God is punishing us by rejecting us, and this creates our spiritual withdrawal. But God *does* understand what we are going through. He is neither rejecting nor punishing us. Cutting ourselves off from God only serves to reinforce our depression.

Just the opposite can also occur. A person may become overinvolved in spiritual things. This could be a compensation for the guilt that he feels. Hours are spent each day in prayer and reading the Scriptures, but it does not lift the depression. This intense activity can actually limit the lifting of our depression, for we are neglecting other areas of our lives which need attention as well.

Perhaps you remember the story of the frog and boiling water. If you drop a frog in a pan of cool water on the stove it begins to swim about. It is enjoying itself. But if you turn on the flame under the pan and gradually warm up the water, the frog is not aware of the change in temperature. He is adjusting to the water as the temperature changes. In time the water becomes very hot, then boiling, and finally the frog is cooked. But the heat comes so gradually and subtly that the frog doesn't realize what is happening until it is too late.

Depression is like that: It is often difficult to detect in its early stages. We may experience some of the symptoms but not understand what they are until they intensify. And when we have moved deeper into depression it is much more difficult to break out of its hold. Notice the three stages of depression described below.

DEPRESSION
Three Intensities

LIGHT	MEDIUM	HEAVY
Low mood	These symptoms intensified	Very intensified
Minor loss of interest	Feelings of hope-lessness	Spiritually either withdrawal or obsessive preoccupation
Thinking okay	Thinking painful and slow	
Knot in stomach	More preoccupied with self	
Eating and sleep-ing okay	Self-blame	
Slight spiritual withdrawal	Eating and sleep-ing a bit disturbed	

DEPRESSION

Light   *Medium*   *Heavy*

Light depression: Your mood may be a bit low or down. There is a slight loss of interest in what you normally enjoy. A few feelings of discouragement may also be present. Your thinking is still normal. There might be a few physical symptoms, but your sleeping and eating habits remain normal. There may be a slight spiritual withdrawal at times.

If you can recognize these symptoms as indications of depression (and if this is a reaction depression), you are still in a position to reverse the depression. Ask yourself these questions: "What is my depression trying to tell me? What may be causing this reaction? What would be the best way to stabilize myself at this time? Would sharing this with another person help, and if so, who will I share this with? What Scriptures would be helpful to read at this time, or what other resource would be helpful?" (Having a pre-planned reading program in mind will be beneficial. This can include a devotional book and specific passages of Scripture. See the suggested passages at the conclusion of this book.) "What type of behaviors or activities would help me at this time?"

Medium depression: All of the above symptoms will be intensified. A prevailing feeling of hopelessness now emerges. Thinking is a bit slow as thoughts about yourself intensify. Tears may flow for no apparent reason. Sleeping and eating problems may emerge—either too much or too little. There is a greater struggle spiritually as the tendency to retreat from God increases. During this type of depression you will probably need the assistance of someone else to handle the depression. But your tendency may be not to share your difficulty with anyone else. This just intensifies your dilemma, however.

Severe depression: All of the previous symptoms occur and are very intense. Personal neglect is very obvious. Appearance and cleanliness are ignored. Shaving or putting on makeup is neglected. It is a chore to complete daily tasks. Spiritual symptoms are obvious—either withdrawal or preoccupation. Crying is frequent, along with intense feelings of dejection, rejection, discouragement, self-blame, self-pity, and guilt. Patterns of eating and sleeping are very disrupted.

A person who recognizes his light or mild depression does not want to have it, but often he does not know how to get rid of it. To keep from going into medium or deep depression it is vital that we "let go" of our depression. Letting go before you plunge into the depths is the key to thwarting long-lasting and heavy depression. To illustrate this, imagine that you are in a pool of deep water holding a heavy rock. The weight of the rock begins to pull you down. "I'm sinking," you say to yourself. What does that thought do to you? It makes you feel even worse. All you are aware of now is the fact that you are sinking lower. In time the surface of the water is over your head. You continue to sink lower and lower and you think, "I'm going down and down and down." This makes you feel worse, which makes you hold onto the rock even more and sink lower, and the vicious circle repeats itself.

Is the problem the fact that you are sinking? No! It is the rock. Let go of the rock, and you then have the opportunity to begin the journey back up to the surface.

Or perhaps you are swimming and you discover that you are a little more tired than you thought you were or that the water is deeper and the current swifter than you expected. By taking action immediately you can quickly head for shore and avert a possible disaster. And hopefully you learn something from the experience. You can take similar action when you are in the light stage of depression.

But if the current is too strong, or if you are totally exhausted and on the verge of drowning, you will need the help of a lifeguard. If you are already in the medium or heavy stage of depression, if your depression has immobilized you and you feel helpless, you need the help of someone who is loving, firm, empathetic, and a good listener to help pull you out of it.

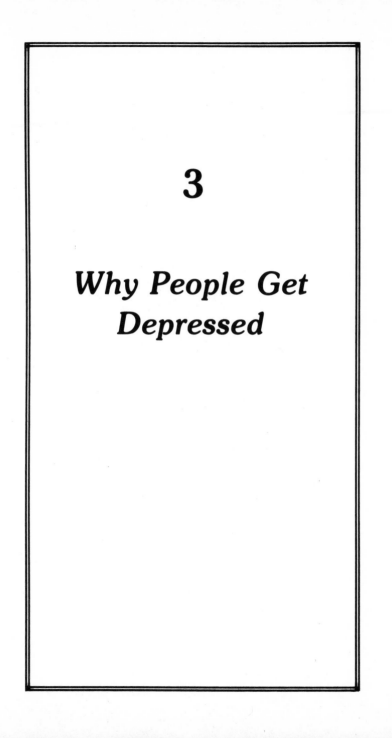

3

*Why People Get
Depressed*

Among the many causes of depression are *issues from our past which still influence us.* One of those issues is deprivation.

An infant is dependent on his mother for physical and emotional care and survival. Mother for the most part gives the child warmth, nourishment, and a gentle fondling. This gives the child a message of love and security. When he has a need, Mother responds. Mother is faithful to his cries, and thus the child learns to trust, for faithful mothering builds trust.

But what happens when the child is repeatedly ignored, or Mother responds but with a lack of love? The child soon learns that Mother and even other people cannot be trusted. He begins to feel neglected and unappreciated. He does not understand the reason, but in his eyes the world appears untrustworthy, undependable, and unloving. These early experiences develop a low frustration level within the child. Who can he trust?

Feelings of resentment and anger develop as seedlings in these early years and persist under the surface into adulthood, making it difficult for him to forgive. Such an experience of deprivation and mistrust often predisposes a person to become depression-prone later in life.[13]

But there are other causes of depression. Such a simple thing as *not eating properly* or *not getting proper rest* can cause depression. The person who does not eat regular meals or get sufficient sleep may find himself becoming depressed because he is cheating his body of the food and rest it needs to keep functioning properly. College students often suffer from this type of depression. The cure is simple and obvious: Eat right and get enough sleep.[14]

This principle is in keeping with the scriptural teaching that the believer's body is the temple of the Holy Spirit. Eating the right type of food and eating it regularly honors the Spirit by properly maintaining His dwelling place. This is fitting in light of our call to present our bodies to Him: "I appeal to you therefore, brethren, and beg of you in view of [all] the mercies of God, to make a decisive dedication of your bodies—presenting all your members and faculties—as a living sacrifice, holy (devoted, consecrated) and well pleasing to God, which is your reasonable (rational, intelligent) service and spiritual worship" (Romans 12:1 AMP).

Reactions to certain drugs can affect a person's moods. Medications administered to correct a physical problem may cause a chemical change in the body bringing on the blues. All drugs affect the body and the mental processes in some way. If a drug results in brain or nervous system toxicity, extreme depression could be the result. If a person takes too much of a drug or sedative over an extended period of time, he may be a candidate for toxic depression. The symptoms are listlessness, indifference, and difficulty in concentrating. Often the person evidences odd and illogical thought patterns which interfere with his normally good judgment. In many cases the depression and drug toxicity will clear up in a day or so after the drug is no longer in the system.[15]

A high school girl who came to me for counseling was quite depressed. For several sessions neither of us could determine the cause until she mentioned that she had gone to her medical doctor a few weeks earlier. She complained of irregularity in her menstrual cycle, so the doctor, in order to regulate it, prescribed birth control pills. A week later the depression hit. After we talked about this the girl went back to the doctor; he had her stop taking the pill. Within days the depression lifted. She was one of those women who cannot take the birth control pill without side effects.

If a person is taking any kind of medication, whether prescribed by a doctor or not, and becomes depressed, he should seek his physician's advice and counsel. The doctor may want to change the dosage or the medication. It is unwise to prescribe medication for oneself.

Our bodies have the potential for creating depression. Our endocrine system includes the various glands which pump hormones into our bloodstream. When there is an imbalance of the hormone level, mood alterations can result. Imbalances of the steroid hormones, which are produced by the adrenal glands, can produce depression. Disorders of the hypothalamus can produce emotional highs and lows.

There are many other physical causes for depression. Infections of the brain or nervous system, generalized body infections, hepatitis, and hypoglycemia can cause depression. Other glandular disorders, such as a low thyroid condition, hyperthyroidism, excessive ovarian hormonal irregularities, and an imbalance of secretions from the adrenal or pituitary glands also cause a type of depression. Usually other symptoms and bodily changes are also in evidence.

The mineral metabolism in our bodies can also affect our moods. We need a balance of minerals such as sodium, potassium, magnesium, and calcium which are called electrolytes. They make up our neurotransmitter system. If nerve A wants to talk to nerve B, an electrical impulse travels down the nerve A cell projection to the nerve cell portion of nerve B. But there is a bit of a gap between nerve A and nerve B. When everything is working correctly the impulse is able to bridge the gap to nerve B and the communication is complete. There are millions of cells in the brain which communicate in this way, and numerous communications can occur each second within the same nerve.

What happens when the mineral metabolism in our bodies gets out of balance? Very simply, either the message being sent from nerve A to nerve B is not strong enough, or it is not being properly sent or received. There are several theories as to why this occurs.

One thoery is related to the amount of stress in our lives. When someone is in a strong emotional state of anger, despair, or anxiety for a relatively long period of time, an excessive amount of adrenaline and other hormones is poured into the bloodstream. It could also be that certain neurotransmitters are manufactured by the body at excessive levels. The result is that the excess biochemicals may change the sensitivity of the nerve receiving the message, or a malfunction could occur at the gap, or the nerves could become exhausted.

What about families where depression seems to be quite prevalent? There may be a genetic defect that has weakened the neurotransmitter system at any one of its points of functioning, making it easier for it to break down. Even if there is no history of depression in the family, some people may have an inborn or acquired weakness of the neurotransmitter system.

This system is strongly affected by diet. The nutrients contained in the food we eat are used for energy and for synthesis of the chemicals needed to maintain and repair the body. Our brain needs these as well, and they are carried to the brain by the bloodstream. Some researchers feel that amino acids and also the B vitamins have a definite effect upon the brain. If you wish additional information on this area, ask your physician to recommend some books on this particular subject.

A book on diet and food allergies that I highly recommend is David Messenger's book, *Dr. Messenger's Guide to Better Health,* published by Revell.

Repressed anger turned inward upon oneself will lead to depression. In fact repressed anger is commonly used as a synonym for depression. This type of anger has been turned from its original source to the inner person. As William Blake wrote in "A Poison Tree":

> I was angry with my friend:
> I was told my wrath, my wrath did end.
> I was angry with my foe:
> I told it not, my wrath did grow.[16]

Reactive depression, usually called *grief depression,* immediately follows the loss of a loved one, a job, or some important opportunity. The intensity of this type of depression is greater immediately after the loss and lessens as the weeks go by. During this time the person's usual functions of living may be impaired, but he can still operate within normal limits. There is a sense of emptiness because of the loss. For the most part, however, his feelings about himself and his self-esteem remain the same. We expect this type of grief depression when a person loses a loved one or even a close friend. Grief is very important in helping a person regain his full functioning capabilities.[17]

Jesus Himself experienced grief depression shortly before His betrayal and crucifixion: "And taking with Him Peter and the two sons of Zebedee, He began to show grief and distress of mind and was deeply depressed. Then He said to them, 'My soul is very sad and deeply grieved, so that I am almost dying of sorrow . . .' " (Matthew 26:37,38 AMP).

Today more and more researchers and writers are emphasizing the role of our *thought life* in causing depression. Faulty and negative thinking is at the root of much depression. This thinking pattern is found in the person who has a low self-concept or self-image. This low self-esteem leads to depression, which reinforces the low self-image and intensifies the depression. It is a vicious cycle at best.

4

The Depressive Triad

To help you understand the thinking process of a depressed person, we will look at three faulty thought patterns which distort the individual's total view of life. We will call this pattern the Depressive Triad.

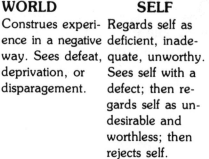

DEPRESSIVE TRIAD
Thinking Patterns

A Negative View Of:

WORLD	SELF	FUTURE
Construes experience in a negative way. Sees defeat, deprivation, or disparagement.	Regards self as deficient, inadequate, unworthy. Sees self with a defect; then regards self as undesirable and worthless; then rejects self.	Anticipates that current difficulties will continue. Sees a future life of hardship, frustration, and deprivation.

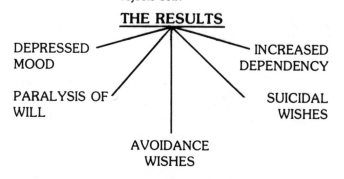

THE RESULTS

DEPRESSED MOOD

INCREASED DEPENDENCY

PARALYSIS OF WILL

SUICIDAL WISHES

AVOIDANCE WISHES

The first part of the Depressive Triad is concerned with a person looking at his experiences in a negative manner. This gives him a negative view of the world. He interprets (rightly or wrongly) his interactions with the world as representing defeat, disparagement, or deprivation. All of life is filled with burdens and obstacles, and his *negative thinking can lead him into depression. When he is depressed he continues to think more and more negatively, which reinforces the depression.*

* The person with a negative view of the world interprets his experiences as actually detracting from himself. Even neutral experiences are interpreted in a negative manner. A neutral attitude on the part of a friend is seen as rejection. A neutral comment is interpreted as a hostile remark. His thinking pattern is clouded by reading into the remarks of other people whatever fits his previously drawn negative conclusions.

He makes assumptions and selective abstractions, generalizing and magnifying events and remarks way out of proportion. He is so predisposed to negative thinking that he automatically makes negative interpretations of situations. Defeat is his watchword.

Our self-talk is the culprit that fosters negative thinking leading to depression, for our thoughts create so many of our feelings. Note the following sequence in the growth of our feelings and behavior.

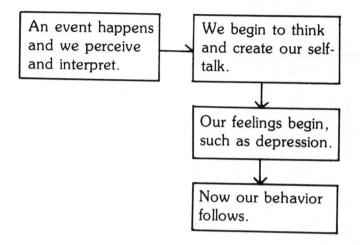

Since self-talk is such an important factor in negative thinking, perhaps that is where we should begin if we are to free ourselves from depression. It is possible to change our self-talk with only a few minutes of effort each day. Spending 15 to 20 minutes a day evaluating and challenging our self-talk can help us create a new pattern of response to life.

The first step is to identify the self-talk and the events which help to create its occurrence. Many of my clients use a journal in which they record at least one event each day. On the following page is an example.

Identify the event (Column A) and record the accompanying emotion or feeling in Column C. Then, as accurately as you can recall, describe your self-talk in Column B. (For now, ignore Column D.) Remember the things that you said to yourself at that time. Often our thoughts and

Date	A. Event	B. Self-Talk	C. Feeling	D. Dispute [18]
9/20	Lost my temper with the kids.	"I shouldn't ever yell at the children; I'm a terrible mother."	Depression.	
9/21	Forgot an appointment with a friend.	"Jim must really be annoyed with me. I'm sure he thinks I'm mad at him and thinks I intentionally stood him up."	Worried and guilty.	
9/22	Attempted to pray.	"God is angry with me or He wouldn't be leaving me feeling so abandoned and unconsoled. This is a sure sign that I'm unforgivably bad; even God has given up on me."	Emptiness, doubt, and guilt.	

beliefs go unnoticed by us. The more hidden and automatic they are, the greater power and influence they have over us. Bringing them into the light of awareness diminishes their power.

When you have identified your self-talk, the next step is to counter it, argue with it, or dispute it. Ask yourself questions such as the following as you complete Column D:

1. Is it possible to rationally support this belief?
2. What evidence is there that this is true?
3. What is the worst possible thing that could occur even if this is true?
4. Is there any reason why I should or must? Whenever you say "should," be sure to ask the question "Why should I?"

More Causes of Depression

Excessive self-pity will also lead to depression. In fact, an overabundance of self-pity indicates poor self-concept. Most of us feel sorry for ourselves at one time or another—that is normal; but to wallow in it is an invitation to depression.

Another common cause of depression has to do with our *behavior*. If the way you are acting is contrary to your moral standards or your value system, depression could be the result. A Christian man who has a high standard of morality but gets involved in an affair could experience depression. A parent who does not live up to his understanding of the scriptural pattern in dealing with his children might wonder why he is depressed. The answer could be in the conflict between the standard he upholds and his actual behavior. When our behavior violates scriptural teaching and then depression results, we may honestly say that sin is the cause of our depression.

Did you know that achieving success can bring on depression? A person works hard, strives for a position, and finally attains his goal. But much to his amazement, he becomes depressed! It could be that all of the emotional and physical energy he exerted has left him depleted. Or it could be that in the new position he feels inadequate and uncertain; the demands for a higher level of performance could be threatening to his confidence and self-esteem. His newly won level of success is not just an achievement, but a new challenge and more work!

Having excessively high standards (being a perfectionist) is a sure way to invite depression into your life. Why? Because of the impossibility of being perfect in this life. It is as though we have two doors to walk through: One is marked "perfectionism" and the other is marked "average" or even "above average." As you open the perfection door you run into obstacle after obstacle which lead directly to a brick wall on the other side. But the average door has no wall on the other side. Those who walk through are led to growth and a balanced life.

We as believers *are* called to be perfect. But

this call to perfection is a call to continued growth and maturity. It does not mean never making an error or a mistake. An objective assessment of ourselves means accepting and recognizing our strengths and talents as well as areas of our lives in which we lack. When we fail to live up to our unrealistic standards we create either anger or depression, or both. Once we become depressed, however, we take just the opposite approach to ourselves: "I can't do anything right. Nothing works for me. I can't even be average."

The best time to work on perfectionistic tendencies is not while you are depressed but at a time when you can be objective about yourself. There are a number of steps to follow in breaking loose from perfectionism.

1. What is your motivation for being a perfectionist? It may help to make a list of the advantages and disadvantages of perfectionism. You may discover (if you're honest with yourself) that the disadvantages actually outweigh the advantages. You may find that you *are* able to accomplish tasks, but in so doing you become tense, irritable, fearful of trying anything new, intolerant of others who do things differently, and depressed when you fail.

2. One of the beliefs that you may have is that unless you aim for perfection you can never be happy; you can't enjoy life or have any satisfaction. unless you attain this goal. Test this belief by using an antiperfectionism form which Dr. David Burns talks about.[19] Record on the form the

actual amount of satisfaction you get from your activities. These could include eating a steak, mowing the lawn, fixing a broken toaster, preparing a talk, washing the car, etc. Then estimate how *perfectly* you did each task (using a scale of 0-100) as well as how *satisfying* each task was (using the same scale).

The purpose of this activity is to show you that your satisfaction is not dependent upon being perfect. Here is an example of a physician who believed that he had to be perfect.

Activity	Record How Effectively You Did This Between 0% and 100%	Record How Satisfying This Was Between 0% and 100%
Fix broken pipe in kitchen.	20% (I took a long time and made a lot of mistakes).	99% (I actually did it!).
Give lecture to medical school class.	98% (I got a standing ovation).	50% (I usually get a standing ovation—I wasn't particularly thrilled with my performance).
Play tennis after work.	60% (I lost the match but played okay).	95% (Really felt good. Enjoyed the game and the exercise).
Edit draft of my latest paper for one hour.	75% (I stuck with it and corrected many errors, and smoothed out the sentences).	15% (I kept telling myself it wasn't the definitive paper and felt quite frustrated).

Talk to student about his career options.	50% (I didn't do anything special. I just listened to him obvious suggestions).	90% (He really seemed to appreciate our talk, so I felt turned on).

3. Are you aware that fear is often a motivating factor in perfectionism? I remember a college student I worked with many years ago who was almost a compulsive perfectionist. He came from a home where you earned love by performing. If you attempted something and failed, then no love was forthcoming. Because of this he ran into difficulties. His fear of failing was also enhanced by obsessive thoughts which interrupted his ability to concentrate. School failure was the worst for him. Thus when he entered college he dropped out of school the first four semesters at final exam time because he did not want to attempt the exams and fail (failure in his eyes was anything less than a strong "A".)

For years he crippled himself with his perfectionism. Fortunately, he received the help he needed through counseling. After he was married and working, he went back to college part-time, willing to do his best and accept whatever he could accomplish. His first 12 courses produced "A's" for him!

These fears often enter our mind automatically. They are part of our deeper hidden self-talk which emerges from time to time as a means of hindering us. Dr. Burns gives the example of a college student who was afraid of submitting a term paper because it had to be "just right." The student was given the suggestion that he list his automatic thoughts and then identify the fear by using the vertical-arrow method. This approach is similar to peeling off the layers of an onion until the origins of the perfectionism are discovered. This process can be very enlightening as deeper fears which have been covered over are discovered. Here is Fred's journey.

Automatic Thoughts	Rational Responses
1. I didn't do an excellent job on the paper. "If that were true, why would it be a problem for me?"	1. All-or-nothing thinking. The paper is pretty good, even though it's not perfect.
2. The professor will notice all the typos and the weak sections. "And why would that be a problem?"	2. Mental filter. He probably will notice typos, but he'll read the whole paper. There are some fairly good sections.
3. He'll feel that I didn't care about it. "Suppose he does. What then?"	3. Mind-reading. I don't know that he will think this. If he did, it wouldn't be the end of the world. A lot of students don't care about their papers.

Automatic Thoughts	**Rational Responses**
	Besides, I do care about it, so if he thought this he'd be wrong.
4. I'll be letting him down. "If that were true and he did feel that way, why would it be upsetting to me?"	4. All-or-nothing thinking; fortune-teller error. I can't please everyone all the time. He's liked most of my work. If he does feel disappointed in this paper he can survive.
5. I'll get a D or an F on the paper. "Suppose I did—what then?"	5. Emotional reasoning; fortune-teller error. I feel this way because I'm upset. But I can't predict the future. I might get a B or a C, but a D or an F isn't very likely.
6. That would ruin my academic record. "And then what would happen?"	6. All-or-nothing thinking; fortune-teller error. Other people goof up at times, and it doesn't seem to ruin their lives. Why can't I goof up at times?
7. That would mean I wasn't the kind of student I was sup-	7. "Should" Statement. Who laid down the rule that I was "sup-

Automatic Thoughts	Rational Responses
posed to be. "Why would that be upsetting to me?"	posed" to be a certain way at all times? Who said I was predestined and morally obliged to live up to some particular standard?
8. People will be angry with me. I'll be a failure. "And suppose they were angry and I was a failure? Why would that be so terrible?"	8. The fortune-teller error. If someone is angry with me, it's his/her problem. I can't be pleasing people all the time—it's too exhausting. It makes my life a tense, constricted, rigid mess. Maybe I'd do better to set my own standards and risk someone's anger. If I fail at the paper, it certainly doesn't make me a failure.
9. Then I would be ostracized and alone. "And then what?"	9. The fortune-teller error. Everyone won't ostracize me!
10. If I'm alone, I'm bound to be miserable.	10. Disqualifying positive data. Some of my happiest times have been when I'm alone. My

Automatic Thoughts	Rational Responses
	"misery" has nothing to do with being alone, but comes from the fear of disapproval and from persecuting myself for not living up to perfectionistic standards.[20]

You know it's not so terrible to be average. The world is composed mostly of average people. Average means that we accept our strengths and weaknesses and try to change the weak areas. As believers we are fortunate in that our attempts at growth are not in our own strength but with the resources of God.

The common thread that underlies much of depression is that of loss. Whenever a person experiences a real or an imagined loss, depression may result. That is why in counseling we search to discover if there has been some loss.

Many losses are perceived as a threat to security or self-esteem, since the object or person lost is viewed as vital for one's existence or day-to-day functioning. It is common for adolescents to undergo bouts of depression because the normal developmental process presents teenagers with many real losses and threats to their self-esteem. They want independence, and yet the loosening of ties to parents and the making of decisions creates anxiety and insecurity.

More and more research is being conducted

on how we respond to loss or even change in our lives. A 1971 issue of *Science Digest* reported on a study conducted by Dr. Eugene S. Pakyel. A total of 373 people were asked to rate the events that would be the most upsetting to them. The 25 most distressing events (and those which can induce a depressive reaction) in order of importance were:

1. Death of a child
2. Death of a spouse
3. Jail sentence
4. Unfaithful spouse
5. Major financial difficulty
6. Business failure
7. Being fired
8. Miscarriage or stillbirth
9. Divorce
10. Marital separation due to an argument
11. Court appearance
12. Unwanted pregnancy
13. Major illness in the family
14. Unemployment for a month. (Additional studies indicated that four out of five marriages end in a divorce when the man is out of work for nine months or more.)
15. Death of a close friend
16. Demotion
17. Major personal illness
18. Start of an extramarital affair
19. Loss of personally valuable objects
20. Lawsuit

21. Academic failure
22. Child married without family approval
23. Broken engagement
24. Taking out a large loan
25. Son drafted

A man might respond to some of these differently from a woman, but these were the most significant events as described by the people in the study. You might discuss these with your family and have each family member make his or her own list. Knowing what distresses a person the most may assist you in responding to him or her in a time of depression.

Reactive depressions are those we experience in our day-to-day living. They involve loss and could even be considered a form of grief. We cannot avoid reactions to the experiences of life, or else we would be robots. Our depression has been designed as a reaction to help us adjust to the changes of life. The key word in reactive depression is *loss*. Any loss must be seen through the eyes of the person who experiences it. The loss will intensify based upon the significance of the object or experience to us. Our attachment and the value we place upon it is correlated with the amount of loss we feel. A person who has a cat or dog as a pet for 12 years may have a considerable attachment to that animal. A non-animal-lover may find it difficult to understand the sense of loss and extent of grief which accompanies the death of the animal. But to the owner of the animal that pet was an integral part of his life and even his family.

An antique vase which has been in the family for 200 years is destroyed. The owner experiences a state of loss or grief for a period of time. He was very attached to that vase because it was a source of memories and sentiment.

There are various types of losses. Dr. Archibald Hart talks about four different types. Think of a time when you may have experienced each type of loss. Perhaps even now you are experiencing one of them.

Abstract losses are intangible, such as the loss of self-respect, love, hope, or ambition. Our minds actually create these losses. We feel that we have experienced this loss. At times the loss may be real, but other times it may not be as bad as we feel it is.

Concrete losses involve tangible objects—the loss of a home, a car, a valued photograph, or a pet. We can feel and see the loss.

Imagined losses are created from our active imaginations. We think someone doesn't like us anymore. We think people are talking behind our backs. Here is where our self-talk is focusing on negatives and our perceptions may not be based on fact.

The most difficult type of loss to handle, however, is the *threatened loss*. This loss has not yet occurred, but there is a real possibility that it will happen. Waiting for the results of a biopsy or a state bar exam, or waiting to hear from the admissions office of a college to which we've applied, carries the possibility of loss. Depression can occur because in this type of loss we are powerless to do anything about it. In a sense we are immobilized.

Any of these losses can happen to us. The depression attached to the loss usually has an appropriate intensity and duration. If the depression lasts longer than seems appropriate, could it be that our attachment to what was lost was too much? It is important at a time when we are not depressed to consider what is important to us. What do we value the most? Are our values in line with scriptural teaching? Modifying our values can benefit our Christian life and can help put our sense of loss in proper perspective.

It is normal to perpetuate our own depression. When we become depressed we tend to do less and think more negatively, which in turn creates more depression. The diagram on the following page illustrates this cycle.

Because of increased depression, our behavior diminishes even more, our negative self-talk increases, and our depression intensifies. If our loss is somewhat abstract or imagined, we may experience other people saying to us, "Snap out of it. What reason do you have to be depressed?" Our reaction to this admonition may be anger— at the lack of understanding on the part of this person, and at ourself for being depressed. But we also feel as though it is out of our control: "I can't really help it. I don't know how to stop it."

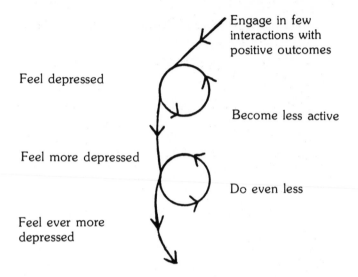

Feel depressed

Engage in few
interactions with
positive outcomes

Become less active

Feel more depressed

Do even less

Feel ever more
depressed

We feel frustrated and blocked, and possibly self-pity sets in as well. All of these thoughts and emotions then lead to the intensification of yet another feeling—loss of control and further loss of self-esteem. All of this deepens our depression.

The Old Testament story of Job gives us in great detail the role that loss plays in bringing on depression. Job experienced loss to a greater degree than most of us will ever experience. He lost his wealth, his means of livelihood, his servants, and his children. Eventually he lost his own physical health and sense of well-being. He experienced the depths of depression. Listen to these complaints of Job:

> Let the day perish wherein I was born, and the night which said, "A manchild is conceived." Let that day be darkness!

Why did I not die at birth, come forth from the womb and expire?
Why is light given to him that is in misery, and life to the bitter in soul, who long for death, but it comes not, and dig for it more than for hid treasures?
For my sighing comes as my bread, and my groanings are poured out like water.
In truth I have no help in me, and any resource is driven from me.
. . . so I am allotted months of emptiness, and nights of misery are apportioned to me. When I lie down I say, "When shall I arise?" But the night is long, and I am full of tossing till the dawn (Job 3:3,4,11,20,21,24; 6:13; 7:3,4 RSV).

There are certain types of losses or events which are common among men. A man's depression is precipitated by financial reversals, failure to achieve a vocational promotion, loss of physical strength, or whatever constitutes his identity.

The events or losses which frequently cause depression in women are different. Major factors are events which affect her identity as a woman, such as a mastectomy or hysterectomy. The feeling of the loss of a significant man in her life, such as father, husband, or boyfriend, is another cause. The loss of a child through death or just the child's normal time of leaving home can create depression. The family life cycle stage of the empty nest is often a depression-filled time for women, who are left feeling empty and alone.

Some fathers experience this loss as well, but many of them simply plunge deeper into their work to overcome their feelings of loss. This tends to make the wife feel even more isolated.

Why do some individuals experience deep depression when losses occur while others experience mild depression or none at all? Are there predisposing factors or personality characteristics involved? Not everyone who experiences a failure, a job loss, or a lack of recognition becomes depressed. Why? What is the difference?

Some studies of depressed individuals have suggested that certain personality characteristics are common to those who experience depression. Of course this would not hold true for everyone, but there are ample indications that these characteristics are usually present.

Studies have found that depressed people are usually perfectionists. They are overly concerned about being on time. They always do the right thing, etc. They have difficulty expressing their emotions and are very rigid. Other studies identified depression-prone people as those who need to gain other people's approval and have very strong lists of shoulds and shouldn'ts. They are overconscientious, continually striving to conform. Some were found to have high needs for order and structure and for others to care for them.

Several studies suggest that the families of depressed individuals are characterized by a high degree of striving for prestige. The children of these families become an instrument for attaining these needs. They learn to push and strive for approval and attention from their parents. Often they transfer this striving for approval to their own friends and school situations and live their lives in competition, always striving for achievement.

Reactive depression associated with marital difficulties is very common. Depression over the end of a love relationship, the loss of a job, disappointment at work, lack of work advancement, financial problems, the breakup of a valued friendship, loss of status, etc. are all understandable. But the breaking of a pencil, the loss of a favorite shirt, or the inability to obtain tickets to an event are not usually events which would precipitate a depression. If they do, there is too high a value attached to them or else there are other stresses and difficulties occurring in the person's life.

Both Moses and Elijah give us clear examples of some of the causes of depression. They especially illustrate the type of thinking pattern which is evident in depression.

> Now Moses heard the people weeping throughout their families, every man at the doorway of his tent; and the anger of the Lord was kindled greatly, and Moses was displeased. So Moses said to the Lord, "Why hast Thou dealt ill with Thy servant? And why have I not found favor in Thy sight, that Thou hast laid the burden of all this people on me? . . . I alone am not able to carry all these people, because it is too

burdensome for me. So, if Thou art going to deal thus with me, please kill me at once, if I have found favor in Thy sight, and do not let me see my wretchedness" (Numbers 11:10,11, 14,15).

Moses was complaining to the Lord, "Why me? Why must I have this burden?" He actually believed that he was carrying the burden himself. At the same time he was also reflecting his feelings of inferiority. It is interesting to note that men can be reluctant to relinquish tasks or authority even though the amount of work they place upon themselves is unbearable. Then because of their inability to delegate, everything looms out of perspective. God dealt with Moses in a very simple manner. He divided up the labor among the elders of Israel. There are times when we wouldn't have to experience depression if we would quit attempting to do it all ourselves and would call for help.

Elijah is a classic example of the tortures of depression. His despondency moved him to the point of wanting to die. (Read the account in 1 Kings 18 and 19.) Elijah is an example of a man who misinterpreted a situation and saw only certain elements of it. He had misconceptions concerning himself, God, and other people. This happened partly because of his tremendous emotional and physical exhaustion.

Elijah had an intense emotional experience in the demonstration of the power of God. Perhaps he expected that everyone would turn to the true

God, and was disappointed when Jezebel was still so hostile. He was physically exhausted because of the encounter on Mount Carmel and his 20-mile race before the king's chariot. When Jezebel threatened his life he became frightened. He probably spent time dwelling upon the threat (and forgetting about God's power which had just been demonstrated). Fearing for his life, Elijah left familiar surroundings and cut himself off from his friends. All of these factors led to his depression. The distortion of his thinking is evident in his lament that he was the only one left, the only one still faithful to God. He was convinced that the whole world was against him. Evidently, his self-pity caused him to lose further perspective.

But the graciousness of the Lord is evident in this account. Nowhere did God berate Elijah for being depressed, or tell him to confess his depression as a sin! Instead, He sent an angel to minister to Elijah. The prophet slept and was given food. God allowed Elijah to "get everything off his chest." The prophet told God his complaint and concern. Then God did two things: He pointed out to Elijah the actual reality of the situation, and He asked Elijah to get into action. He gave him an assignment. This account of Elijah helps us to see the various causes of depression; it also gives us an insight as to how God responds to a depressed person.

After considering the many things that can cause it, you may feel that depression is a complex condition! Yes, it can be, especially when several of the causes work together to develop the depression. But depression does not have to be the end of the world, even though to the depressed individual it appears that way. There are ways to cope with and counteract the causes of depression. It can be an opportunity for change and growth as the causes are pinpointed and steps taken to rebuild the areas of life that are causing problems.

Is it possible that some people benefit from depression and don't want to give it up?

Yes, it is. A housewife might use her depression, even though it hurts, to gain attention and sympathy from her husband. If she notices an increase in attentiveness during her bouts of depression, she might tend to resist giving up the depression. She may feel that the pain of depression is worthwhile because of her husband's response. A husband may avoid taking responsibility in the family by being depressed.

A salesman came to me for counseling because of extensive depression. He hadn't made a sale in six weeks; when he arrived at the office each morning, instead of making 30 or so phone calls, as he usually did, he would sit there staring at the wall and sensing his depression.

At the end of the day he would go home for the night and still be depressed. The next morning the same pattern was repeated. One day he admitted that in a sense he liked his depression because it numbed him to the pain of not making any sales, and he could also use the depression as an excuse for not selling.

A housewife admitted in counseling that she felt her depression was her way of getting back at her husband for being such a rotten person. She seemed to enjoy the pain and upset her depression caused him. This newly discovered weapon was so effective that she was hesitant to give it up.

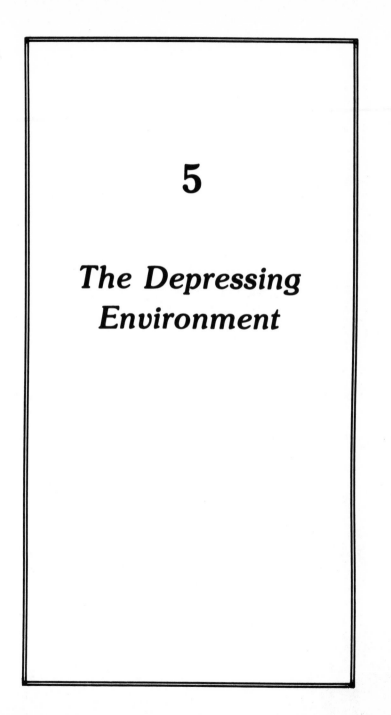

5

*The Depressing
Environment*

A person is largely responsible for his own emotions, but can one family member cause depression in another? Could a person help to create an environment that would tend to bring on someone else's depression?

Yes, it is possible to create what is called a depressogenic environment, one that does not provide a person with adequate support for his self-esteem. In most cases this environment undermines self-esteem or else elicits emotions and conflicts that the person cannot handle without becoming depressed. Constant attack by someone whom we love and respect can bring on feelings of hurt, guilt, and helplessness which can lead to depression.

This type of environment is contrary to the teaching of Scripture that all believers are members of the body of Christ. As believers we are to encourage, to edify, and to build up one another. We have been called to love one another. Especially in the marriage relationship, love is to be a sacrificial, servanthood type of love.

Colossians 3:21 states: "Fathers, do not provoke or irritate or fret your children—do not be hard on them or harass them, lest they become discouraged and sullen and morose and feel inferior and frustrated; do not break their spirit" (AMP). Proverbs 11:29 says: "The fool who provokes his family to anger and resentment will finally have nothing worthwhile left. He shall be the servant of a wiser man" (TLB).

In a depressogenic environment the thousands of negative verbal and nonverbal exchanges can affect the vulnerable person. I am not saying that the depressed person is not responsible for his depression but that the environment in which he lives can get the process started. Some people are more vulnerable than others to such an environment.

The tactics most commonly employed in families to induce depression are identified on the list that follows. Use this list to evaluate the atmosphere of your own home. If any of these are present, take steps immediately to correct them. This could be done by confronting family members with their actions; talking to a friend, pastor, or counselor; or getting books and other resources to help counteract depressogenic behaviors.

Without being facetious, here are the ten most powerful ways to help a family member become depressed:

1. Try to control the other person so he cannot gain any type of independence. The control may be subtle or overt, but you direct his life for him. Eventually this leads him to believe that he cannot exist without your direction.

2. Try to convince the other person that he

needs you and could not survive without your emotional support.

3. Give your spouse or child ambivalent messages that undermine self-esteem, such as, "In spite of how sloppy you are, I still love you," or, "I guess this is just the burden that I have to bear, having a child (or a husband) like you. But I still do care for you."

4. Try to provoke guilt by making the other person feel responsible for situations or conditions. Make him feel miserable. This can be done without ever saying a word. A housewife once reflected how she felt when her husband would come home and, without saying a word, would look around the house to see if it were clean, and then would cast a disgusted look her way. She was a neat housekeeper, but he was a perfectionist. With a look and with silence the rest of the evening he successfully conveyed to her his annoyance.

5. Misinterpret the person's intentions and motives so that he begins to doubt his own perceptions. This can be done by constantly questioning: "Are you sure you did that or said that?" or, "I don't think anyone else heard you say that. . ." or, "You don't really mean that—you're just saying it because. . ." After a while the person may begin to doubt himself.

6. Make sure the communication process is blocked. This is the surest way to reject a person and also to build indifference in a relationship. Remain silent, or just respond on a cliche level,

with no deep feeling. Creating an atmosphere where people cannot express true feelings or ideas destroys relationships.

7. Insert competitiveness into the family relationships. Anything that can be done to build envy and jealousy will have a detrimental effect upon the family. Compare one child with another, or give more attention to one child to get back at your spouse.

8. Maintain a monotonous environment, without any joy or humor. As people share funny experiences or their delight in events, but receive no positive response, they begin to wonder about themselves; eventually they quit sharing.

9. Refuse any show of emotions, especially healthy reactions to anger. Do not allow the other family members to express their emotions. As they learn to bottle up their anger, one of the best outlets or channels for it will be depression.

10. Become depressed yourself to express some indirect anger toward the other person. Try to make him feel confused and helpless.[21]

As you can see, the items on the list do nothing to build confidence and self-esteem. And yet these conditions exist in many homes. Are people in your home depressed? If you identified with all or part of the list, please talk your situation over with other family members. Take the necessary steps to build a healthy atmosphere in your home in which it would be difficult to become depressed because of the environment.

Today we hear so much about a new phenomenon called "burnout." Is this a form of depression? Does it cause depression? How do the two relate? More and more literature is being written each year to attempt to explain the causes and characteristics of this condition. It appears that during the past 20 years we have developed a new vocabulary in order to explain what is happening to mankind— words such as *stress, midlife crisis,* and now *burnout.*

Here is a simple overall definition of burnout: "To deplete oneself. To exhaust one's physical and mental resources. To wear oneself out by excessively striving to reach some unrealistic expectation imposed by one's self or by the values of society."[22] Burnout is a complex process which involves all five major areas of our life: physical, intellectual, emotional, social, and spiritual.

The physical aspect refers to the amount of energy available to do what one needs to do and wants to do. Burnout's first symptom is an all-around feeling of fatigue. Usually people suffering from burnout are not involved in exercises or in a nutrition or stress-reduction program.

The intellectual aspect refers to the sharpness with which a person thinks and solves problems. In burnout this ability diminishes. Creativity diminishes, cynicism increases concerning new approaches, and there is no hobby or means of intellectual relaxation.

The emotional aspect refers to whether the person's emotional life is basically positive or negative. Is the person optimistic or pessimistic about what is occurring in his or her life? Are there emotional outlets available other than work? Is the person aware of what is happening to him emotionally? If the person is overinvested in work, and then his work begins to deteriorate, the person's whole life can begin to go downhill. Depression can set in because of the loss of dreams and expectations which have been so tied into his work. People with a balanced life of outside interests have a buffer against burnout.

The social aspect of burnout refers to feelings of involvement compared to feelings of isolation. A major question is, "What kind of social support system does one have?" Does he feel free to share his feelings of frustration, anger, fatigue, or disillusionment? Does he have anyone who will listen? Unfortunately, when a person is experiencing burnout he often does not want to burden anyone else with his problems, thus creating further isolation.

The spiritual aspect refers to the degree of meaning that a person has in his or her life. If a person's expectations concerning his work have been dashed, he begins to feel a void in his life. His dream about life or even expectations about what God was supposed to do for him may be a source of disappointment.

Some burnout can be simply physical. A person is tired of his job, of the hours, or of the ineffectiveness of the system. Usually he recovers after a short vacation or even just a day off. Any type of change which brings about a new interest or even variations of his work routine may help.

The major symptom of burnout is the most serious, and it can happen to Christians and non-Christians alike. This is long-term, and it is the *psychological* functioning, which includes the intellectual, emotional, social, and spiritual aspects. There is a decline in happiness, empathy, sensitivity, and compassion. This burnout occurs gradually and is noticeable when a crisis occurs. The relationships in all areas of life are affected. Recreation becomes mechanical. The person is aloof and distant with friends, holds his emotions inside, and is insensitive to family members.

Psychological burnout takes longer to occur and also longer to reverse. Days off or vacations or a one-day seminar on stress or burnout are not enough. Time and a reorientation to life is what is needed. A spiritual renewal through the Word, prayer, and close Christian friends will also be part of the cure. Part of the reversal also involves looking at the work environment to see if it has contributed to the deterioration. But the real problem isn't circumstances as such but our response to circumstances. The Word of God clearly tells us that we will not be free of problems just because our circumstances are calm and peaceful. The promise of peace is a learned response which comes from application of God's Word in the midst of difficulty.

If you want a simple explanation of how people respond in a burnout, just analyze the word itself. The word "burn" brings about the vision of heat, fire, conflagration, or anger. Some people become angry at their jobs, their family, their friends, or their employer. This is an anger which is just seething beneath the surface, ready to boil and spill over at the slightest provocation.

The second part of the word is "out." There is nothing left. It is as though the person has checked out of life itself. He gives up, claiming that nothing can be done and that the entire mess is hopeless. He hurts others by doing nothing. His energy, integrity, care, love, and desire are gone.

What causes burnout? Is it a disease with germs carried about by the winds of life? Where does it originate? There are numerous causes, but two of the major ones are expectations and distribution. Unrealistic expectations about life, people, or an occupation can lead to burnout. Some individuals focus upon the goal that they wish to accomplish with no regard to the struggle involved in the attainment process.

Many individuals are unaware of the realities of an occupation with its pain and struggle. Their dreams of changing the world can be shattered easily. When they realize that they will not be able to change the system, idealism turns to cynicism.

Another contributing factor is the belief that "it can't happen to me." Other people collapse, but not me. Other people fail, but not me. Other people burn out, but not me.

The second major contributor to burnout is distribution.

Many persons seem to fall into a metaphor of life that might be characterized by one of two geographic phenomena: One is Death Valley, and the other is the Dead Sea.

Death Valley is a desert. It is interesting because it was once an ocean teeming with life. It supported vast societies, giving life to creatures and life forms no longer present on the planet. It gave all of that for untold eons. But something changed. Oceans need feeding. Water flows from somewhere to give life to the ocean so that it might in turn give life. Whatever fed the ocean that became Death Valley stopped. Although there was nothing coming in, the ocean still tried to feed the societies that depended on it for life. It gave so much that it dried up and became not an ocean but a desert. Death Valley is a phenomenon of nature in which there is an outlet but no inlet. It simply gave up what it had and, since nothing new was coming in, it died.

Think how that might describe some people. They are asked to give of themselves day in and day out. Teachers, social workers, ministers, and police officers all have demands made on them by others. If they believe that they can continually give without somehow being fed themselves, then they become psychological Death Valleys, unable to give anymore. They become hollow, drained, sterile. They are the teachers without life in them. Their classrooms are infertile. They are incapable of creating a climate in which young things can grow. They are the fathers whose kisses are always dry; they are unable to give the warm, wet kisses of affection that enable their families to grow and develop. They are persons who have no sustenance coming in from outside themselves. They have dried up.

The Dead Sea is a body of water that is stagnant. The Jordan River flows into the Dead Sea. It was once a body of water that supported life, but it no longer does so. It has an inlet but no outlet. It collects the waters of the Jordan River, accepts life, and then doesn't let it out again, with the result that it is smothered and dies. Nothing escapes from the Dead Sea. It has nowhere to go. It takes everything in but lets nothing out.

There are people who, for one reason or another, are unable to let anything out. There are people who have more than they need. They have no ability to share the richness of themselves. They collect their emotions and hold them in. Never getting out, those feelings fester, become cancerous, and eat away, so that the persons again become devoid of life. They bloat with collected human expressions, experiences, joys, and sadnesses. They don't know how to give. They are the physicians who are unable to reach out a hand to a dying patient. They are the athletes who forever pretend that they are on the playing field and never come to the rest of life. They are the nurses who tell little boys that cuts and broken arms don't hurt because all of their own feelings have been smothered in their own internal Dead Sea.

They take everything and they give nothing back.[23]

What can help? We need expectations and hopes for our lives. But if we learn to avoid expectations which set us up for failure, we will achieve a better balance. If we can avoid distribution systems which are draining or which create isolation, we will be maintaining a better balance.

Depression can take many forms; there is a difference between general depression and the type of depression which indicates burnout. In general depression, the condition invades all areas of a person's life. In burnout, depression is usually temporary, specific, and even localized. It is involved with just one area of a person's life. A person may be downcast and despondent on the job but can go home and swim or enjoy racquetball. In general depression, the individual is more likely to feel guilt; in burnout the strong emotion is anger.

The real problem in depression, however, is nonfeeling. When the symptoms are obvious and the person denies that anything is wrong, an "I-don't-care" attitude begins to emerge. It is sometimes difficult to distinguish between the depression of burnout and general depression, since both have an "I-don't-care" response. As has already been mentioned, however, the depression of burnout is usually localized and short-lived.

6

Where Is God When I'm Depressed?

Isaiah 43:1-3 says, "But now [in spite of the past judgments for Israel's sins] thus says the Lord Who created you, O Jacob, and He Who formed You, O Israel: Fear not, for I have redeemed you —ransomed you by paying a price instead of leaving you captives; I have called you by your name, you are Mine. When you pass through the waters I will be with you, and through the rivers they shall not overwhelm you; when you walk through the fire you shall not be burned or scorched, nor shall the flame kindle upon you. For I am the Lord your God, the Holy One of Israel, your Savior; I give Egypt [to the Babylonians] for your ransom, Ethiopia and Seba [a province of Ethiopia] in exchange for your release" (AMP).

This Scripture is very comforting and at the same time deals with a misconception that believers often hold. Many people feel that being a Christian is an insurance policy against everyday difficulties and emotional problems. This verse does not say that we will go around or above the fire or water, but that as we go through it God is with us! In the midst of difficulty it is possible to learn peace and contentment.

Elizabeth Skoglund, in her book *The Whole Christian*, says:

Many Christians seem to think that they are always to be the opposite of depressed, that is, happy and joyful. The rightness or wrongness of that viewpoint lies in one's definition of those words. A light sort of continued "up" feeling is not, in my opinion, what God expects of us; and to teach that this is a necessary characteristic of a good Christian is to cause great discouragement and guilt. What God does give to a Christian is a settled sense of contentment. One person who has suffered greatly said with tears: "I am glad God has used my pain to bring something good into this world, and if I could choose to change it all and lose the good, I would not change even the pain. But I did not like the pain nor do I like it now." She was content but not masochistically happy over suffering. At times she had been depressed and frightened, but never had she lost that deep sense of God's control and strength in her life. Such an attitude reminds one of Paul's words: "We are troubled on every side, yet not distressed; we are perplexed, but not in despair; persecuted, but not forsaken; cast down, but not destroyed" (II Cor. 4:8,9 KJV).[24]

A depressed person might read this account and say, "But that's not me. I'm not content with my depression" and begin to feel worse. Remember, it takes time to arrive at that point. It does not happen overnight. But it is possible! When you are depression-prone you need to develop a sense of God's great love for you. The following paraphrase of 1 Corinthians 13, titled

"Because God Loves Me," will help you "tune in" to God's love. Read the paraphrase out loud every morning and evening. Concentrate on the words. Read with meaning and emphasis. As you hear your own voice stating the facts about God's love, gradually the realization of that love will seep into your life.

BECAUSE GOD LOVES ME
1 Corinthians 13:4-8

Because God loves me He is slow to lose patience with me.

Because God loves me He takes the circumstances of my life and uses them in a constructive way for my growth.

Because God loves me He does not treat me as an object to be possessed and manipulated.

Because God loves me He has no need to impress me with how great and powerful He is because He is God, nor does He belittle me as His child in order to show me how important He is.

Because God loves me He is for me. He wants to see me mature and develop in His love.

Because God loves me He does not send down His wrath on every little mistake I make, of which there are many.

Because God loves me, He does not keep score of all my sins and then beat me over the head with them whenever He gets the chance.

Because God loves me He is deeply grieved when I do not walk in the ways that please Him, because He sees this as evidence that I don't trust Him and love Him as I should.

Because God loves me He rejoices when I experience His power and strength and stand up under the pressures of life for His Name's sake.

Because God loves me He keeps on working patiently with me even when I feel like giving up and can't see why He doesn't give up with me, too.

Because God loves me He keeps on trusting me when at times I don't even trust myself.

Because God loves me He never says there is no hope for me; rather, He patiently works with me, loves me, and disciplines me in such a way that it is hard for me to understand the depth of His concern for me.

Because God loves me He never forsakes me even though many of my friends might.

Because God loves me He stands with me when I have reached the rock bottom of despair, when I see the real me and compare that with His righteousness, holiness, beauty, and love. It is at a moment like this that I can really believe that God loves me.

Yes, the greatest of all gifts is God's perfect love![25]

7

What To Do About Depression

If you find that you are becoming or are already depressed, what can you do about it? Should you let your husband or wife know?

Let's talk about what you can do if you find yourself becoming depressed. First of all, check for any physical reasons for your depression. You may even want to see your medical doctor. If there is no physical cause, then your next step is to ask yourself two key questions. You may even want to ask your mate or a good friend to help you think them through.

1. What am I doing that might be bringing on my depression? (Check your behavior to determine that it is consistent with Scripture. Ask yourself if you are doing anything to reinforce the depression.)

2. What am I thinking about or in what way am I thinking that might be making me depressed?

If your thinking pattern is negative and you persist in making negative value judgments about yourself, you can break this pattern. First, recognize and identify the thoughts that you express to yourself. When something happens and you experience depression, you need to realize that there is more than the outward event behind your feelings. Perhaps you had a negative thought or made a negative value judgment regarding the thing that happened. This sets you up for depression.

Second, realize that many of your thoughts are automatic. They are involuntary. You don't have to think about having them—they just pop in. They are not the result of deliberation or reasoning. But if you reason against them you can put them aside.

Third, distinguish between ideas and facts. You may think something, but that does not mean that it is true. If you feel that your spouse does not like the way you dress or the meals you cook, check it with him. You may be right, but you could also be wrong. If you make an assumption, always try to see if it is true.

Finally, after you have discovered that a particular thought is not true, state precisely why it is inaccurate or invalid. This step is vital! Putting the reasons into words helps you in three ways: It actually reduces the frequency of the ideas coming back; it decreases the intensity of the idea; and it tones down the feeling or mood that the idea generates. The more you counteract some of your ideas in this manner the more your depression is lessened.

Watch any assumptions or generalizations that you make. Learn to say to yourself, "I'm jumping to a conclusion again," or, "I exaggerated again," or, "I assumed that she didn't like it—but it could just as well be true that she did like it." Strange as it seems, it is important for you (when you are alone, of course) to do this aloud; you need to hear your own voice expressing this idea. Your thinking pattern *can* be changed.

Second Timothy 1:7 says: "For God did not give us a spirit of timidity—of cowardice, of craven and cringing and fawning fear—but [He has given us a spirit] of power and of love and of calm and well-balanced mind and discipline and self-control" (AMP).

Ephesians 4:23 says: "Be constantly renewed in the spirit of your mind—having a fresh mental and spiritual attitude" (AMP).

Second Peter 1:13 says: "I think it right, as long as I am in this tabernacle (tent, body), to stir you up by way of remembrance" (AMP).

We are called upon to change our thinking pattern or our thought life; but the Scripture also states (Romans 12:2; Ephesians 4:23) that the Holy Spirit is actively at work in influencing our minds and helping us to control our thoughts.

Here are two suggestions that have helped many people to change their thought life from a negative pattern to a positive one. A physician asked a patient to keep a stopwatch with him and to start it when he had a negative thought and stop it when a positive thought came in to replace it. He noted the blocks of time on a sheet of graph paper, and carried the watch and the paper with him wherever he went. Before this experiment, he felt that the negative thoughts were in his mind constantly. By timing them and putting them on a graph he found that they did not occur as often as he thought. The whole process of timing the thoughts helped him to develop methods of controlling the negative thoughts he did have. He began to take control of his life again.

Another method of breaking a negative thinking pattern involves writing Philippians 4:6 on a 3x5 card: "Do not fret or have any anxiety about anything, but in every circumstance and in everything by prayer and petition [definite requests] with thanksgiving continue to make your wants known to God" (AMP). On the other side of the card write the word "STOP." Whenever you are struggling with the negative thinking, take out the card. Hold it with the word "STOP" facing you and say the word out loud. Turn the card over and read the Scripture out loud. If you are at work or with other people you may read silently. Do this regularly, and you will defeat the negative thought pattern and replace it with the positive thoughts of the Scriptures.

Positive Steps

Begin your positive steps in overcoming depression by asking yourself these three questions:

1. What is my depression doing for me? Am I getting anything out of being depressed?

2. Have I undergone any major changes or stresses during the past few months or years? What are they? How am I trying to adjust to them?

3. What kind of environment am I in? Is it helping me to come out of my depression, or

could it be making me more depressed?

Then undertake the following additional steps.

1. Look at your eating and sleeping habits to see if these ought to be changed.

2. Are you following your normal routine of life or are you withdrawing by staying in bed longer, staying away from friends, letting the dishes stack up in the sink, and avoiding regular activities? Are you cutting yourself off from your friends and family? If so, it is important to force yourself to stay active, as hard as it might seem. Remember that a depressed person begins behaving and acting in such a way that the depression is reinforced. You must break the depressive pattern of behavior by yourself or by asking someone to help you.

3. Let your mate know that you are depressed. Ask him to listen to you as you explain it. If you want him to comment, let him do so; but if not, tell him you'd rather he didn't. If you are angry with him, or with anyone, discuss your feelings with the person and get them out into the open.

4. Each day, either by yourself or with another person's help, make a list of what you would do during the day if you were not depressed. After you have made this list in detail, work out a plan to follow what is on that list each day.

Another way of developing a pattern of positive behavior is to make an extensive list (with help if necessary) of Pleasant Events. After the list is made, select several events to do each day. This Pleasant Events schedule is not a panacea for all depression, but often you can break the pattern of depression through your behavior. Most people feel better when they engage in pleasant activities.

5. Be sure to read the books suggested in the study portion of this book. These will assist you in developing a thinking pattern that could lift your depression. Focusing and dwelling upon positive Scriptures will also help you. Each morning read these passages; put them on posters and place them around the house: Psalm 27:1-3; 37:1-7; Isaiah 26:3; 40:28-31.

Is it possible to pray one's way out of depression? Many individuals have tried to do so but found no change. It depends upon the type or cause of depression. If sin is the direct cause of depression, then prayer which includes confession, repentance, and the acceptance of forgiveness can rid you of the depression. But all too often a depressed individual *thinks* his depression is caused by sin when in reality it is not. This is often a reflection of the person's feeling of worthlessness which accompanies depression.

Some people advocate praising God as a means of defeating depression. Genuine praise for who God is and the strength that He gives us can be an aid in handling our depression. However, waiting until we feel like praising Him will hamper us, for in a depressed state we probably do not feel full of praise. Taking the time and energy to sit and list our blessings and then specifically mentioning them to God in prayer may give us a better perspective. The best way of doing this is with another person who is not depressed and knows your life quite well.

When you are experiencing depression, one of the best remedies is to become more active. Changing one's level of activity has several benefits, but it is often difficult. It means going counter to what you are feeling. The first step in increasing your activity is to discover the good reasons which are strong enough to make you try. Secondly, you will need to challenge the thoughts and ideas which you are using or will use to keep you from being active.

Increasing your activity is a definite way of changing your thinking. When you do less you think of yourself as inadequate, lazy, and worthless. A good reason to become more active is to challenge those ideas; by being more active you create evidence that you are not like that. You show yourself that you can get started and accomplish something.

Studies indicate that activity will improve your mood. Usually the more you do the better you feel. It also provides a helpful diversion from your depression by distracting your mind from unpleasant thoughts.

Activity will also counteract the fatigue which you find with depression. It is a paradox with depression that when you are depressed you need to do more to gain more energy. When you are not depressed, you are revived by rest and inactivity. Studies also show that activity will increase our motivation. By completing a simple task successfully, you will be motivated to try some other task. With depression there is another seeming paradox—you must do what you don't feel like doing before you will feel like doing it! This is strange, but true. And this phenomenon is not limited to a depressed state, for many people find that by doing a behavior first, their feelings come in line with that behavior.

By being active you can stimulate yourself to think. Thus your mental ability is stimulated as well. New solutions to previously unsolvable situations are discovered.

When you become more active you find that other people positively reinforce what you are doing. You no longer have to hear them suggest that you "do something."

The following is an activity record to help keep track of your activities. This written exercise is important because when you are depressed you do not remember the positive as well as the negative. Selective remembering is in progress. Be aware of what you write. You may tend to write down a negative, such as "I just did nothing." But perhaps your doing nothing involved watching a TV program and drinking a cup of tea. Record that activity instead, since that is doing something. Record hour by hour what you do for a week. Next to the actual activity indicate how much satisfaction you felt on a scale from 0 to 5 (0 meaning none and 5 meaning great!). This tabulation can help you see what it is that gives you pleasure and satisfaction.

Weekly Activity Schedule[26]

	M	T	W	Th	F	S	Su
9-10							
10-11							
11-12							
12-1							
1-2							
2-3							
3-4							
4-5							
5-6							
6-7							
7-8							
8-12							

It is also important for you to plan an actual schedule of what you will do. By scheduling your activities you are once more taking control of your life. It will also help you overcome indecisiveness, which is a common characteristic of depression. Keeping a schedule and scheduling activities will give you an opportunity to identify and counter self-defeating thoughts which keep you immobilized. By reviewing what you have already done and by looking over what you plan to do the next day, you will begin to have a different set of feelings about yourself. Here is an example of a woman who was interested in going back to college to take some classes. Listed below are her thoughts and answers to the thoughts.

Ways to Keep Yourself Passive and Answers to Them[27]

Thoughts	*Answers*
It's too hard to find out about taking classes.	It's as difficult as it is—no more, no less. I've done many more difficult things.
I won't know what schools to call or what questions to ask.	The idea is to do it—not do it perfectly. It's better to do a poor job, to try to find out, than not to try at all.
I don't want to do it. I hate making phone calls.	That's what I think now—but earlier I wanted to. So whether or not I want to do it now is irrelevant. I'd better do it now for my own good.
I don't think I'm up to doing it. I'll wait until I feel more like doing it.	I don't know for sure. I'm not a mind reader. I'll experiment and see what I can do. Inspiration comes from activity, not the other way around.
I've wasted so much time already. When I start to	I didn't waste time. I just did something different

do it, it reminds me of wasted time.	with that time. Now the question is, What do I want to do with this time—more of the same or something different?
I can't decide which school to call first.	Call the one that comes first in alphabetical order. Calling the least helpful is better than not calling one at all.

How do you plan this schedule? Very simply. Be flexible; and don't set it up in a rigid pattern so you cannot make changes. Stick with the general plan. If you miss an acitvity, just let it go and schedule it another time. If you finish a task early, don't start the next task until the set time. Do something enjoyable until that time. Treat yourself! Schedule activities in half-hour and one-hour intervals, and don't plan activities that are too specific or too general. Don't bite off more than you can chew. Enjoying the activity at a satisfying pace is part of the plan.

If you have let the house go for several weeks, it may take several weeks or days to establish some order. That extended time is all right! Break your tasks down into smaller tasks. Grade them from easy to difficult. List the various jobs which need to be done, whether your task is to clean the basement, the yard, or the living room. List what you will do within that overall job. Cleaning the living room may involve picking up all the magazines, dusting, vacuuming, washing the two windows, getting the dog hair off the easy chair, etc.

Don't be surprised if you are tempted to skip scheduling your activities. Here are some typical sabotage techniques you may try to use on yourself and some ways to counter them.

Statement: "I don't know if I can think of any activities to schedule."

Answer: You are probably having trouble thinking of any. Why not list activities that you must do each day (such as eating and dressing), activities that give you pleasure, and activities that bring a sense of accomplishment?

Statement: "I have never kept records and I have never been able to work under a schedule."

Answer: Scheduling is a simple skill which can be learned. If it is difficult to keep an hour-by-hour schedule you could list one task from 8:00-10:00, another from 10:00-12:00, and one between 1:00-6:00. This is a good way to begin.

Statement: "I have so much difficulty with distractions. I just do not follow through."

Answer: Make a list of the typical distractions. Identify what they are, and then in writing formulate how you will refuse to give in to that distraction. You may need to unplug the TV, phone, and home computer and reconnect them when the task is completed. It is also all right to tell a caller that you are busy but will talk to him or her at a later time. Write yourself a contract such as "I will complete 30 minutes of house-cleaning and then read *Redbook* for 20 minutes."

Use signs around the house to remind you of your commitments and schedule. Make them odd and different in order to attract your attention. When you start a task, select the easiest and simplest so that you are almost guaranteed success.

8

Help From Medications

Medication is one of the forms of treatment for depression. Research in the use of drugs for depression started in the 1950s when some physicians noticed that patients being given a drug for tuberculosis experienced an improvement in their mood. They also experienced a greater sense of well-being and more energy. From there researchers began to investigate more thoroughly, which led to the first antidepressant drugs, known as the "MAO" inhibitors.

Since then a number of medications in the MAO group have been developed. Some of the more frequently used are Nardil, Marplan, Niamis, Parnate, and Eutonyl. It is believed that their antidepressant effect is created by altering and balancing the levels of neurotransmitters in the brain. Like all of the antidepressant medications, they can be obtained only by a doctor's prescription and should be used only if a doctor recommends them.

A second type of drugs is used more frequently than the MAO group. These have been called the "tricyclics." The most common (by brand name) are the following: Tofranil, Elavil, Pertofrane, Aventyl, Pamelor, Vivactil, and Sinequan. These drugs are thought to correct the biochemical imbalances which are involved in endogenous depression.

Drugs are used mostly in the more severe types of depressions and those whose origins are physical. They are not usually used, nor are they very helpful, in reactive depressions (unless the reactive depression has lingered so long that it has begun to affect the physical system). These drugs may be useful. There are some depressions that are reactive in nature in which the body's chemical balance must be restored for recovery to occur.

Most prescribed medications need about 10 to 14 days for them to really take effect. It is important for a person not to give up too soon when using such medications. If there is no improvement after three or four weeks, the physician may want to switch to another medication.

Each person is different and may respond in a different way to the medication. The side effects could threaten the depressed individual. Many medications produce side effects, even cold and allergy medicines. Dry mouth, drowsiness, a drop in blood pressure, water retention, constipation, and sweating are but a few of the side effects. The effects tend to be mild, and most clear up in a few days or weeks. Continued side effects need to be reported to your medical doctor.

It is important to let your doctor do the actual prescribing and to make any changes in dosage. Too often well-meaning friends and relatives have their own opinions about the use of proper medication. In using medication it is important to follow professional guidelines.

Another caution is in order. It is possible to encounter a physician who believes that medication is the only treatment for depression, and that counseling or therapy offer little or no help. I would recommend asking for other opinions, because therapy is one of the main treatment forms for depression. In some cases a combination of medication and therapy is used, and in other cases therapy by itself.

Taking medication is not an admission that one is "mentally ill." This idea makes some people resist taking medication. Another concern about medication is the possibility of addiction. These modern medications do not produce addiction or physical dependence. One of the reasons for this is that tricyclics and MAO inhibitors do not have any mood effects on "normal" people who do not have the biochemical imbalances of depression. Unlike "speed" and illegal drugs on the street today, you cannot get "high" on anti-depressants. God uses many means to bring us out of depression, including therapy, prayer, reading, exercise, and medication.

The Exercise Approach

Exercise is an active approach to life whereas depression is a malady which creates passivity. Inactivity gradually becomes the style of life. Exercise not only can be partial inoculation against depression, but it can also be part of the treatment. Active people or those who engage in regular exercise each week report a better sense of psychological well-being than those who do not exercise.

Dr. Otto Appenzeller of the University of New Mexico has found that the nervous system releases hormones called catecholamines during marathon running. In his research project he discovered that the catecholamines in all marathon runners were increased to 600 percent above normal. It is also known that these hormones are low in people suffering from depression. Therefore it would appear that the connection between running and the release of these hormones could be generalized to include moderate forms of exercise.[28]

In another experimental study a number of depressed clients became involved in a gradual planned program of running. They reported reduced tension and sleep improvement, and depressive symptoms began to lift.[29]

Are there other reasons in addition to hormonal changes which could account for the lifting of depression through exercise? Yes, there are. The fact of participating in a pleasant activity can assist one's outlook. A sense of success and mastery can develop as the person continues with his exercise program. Factors such as self-discipline, patience, and endurance can be reinforcing to a person's self-image. And because exercise is active, it counteracts the passivity and helplessness of depression. Before engaging in any type of exercise program a person needs to have a physical checkup, engage in a program which he could learn to enjoy, and move into it gradually.

I did not really have a regular exercise program until 1980, when I experienced a stress reaction or burnout. During that time I was also depressed. My physician told me that there wasn't much wrong with me except that I was like a one-ton truck trying to do the work of a two-ton truck. I didn't need a major overhaul but a minor tune-up. He also had the audacity to tell me that the only other thing that was wrong with me was that I had 12 extra pounds! His words were the extra push I needed to get into action.

Gradually I lost 18 pounds, began to ride an indoor bicycle, and with the encouragement of two friends learned to play racquetball. Now I ride an indoor bicycle ten miles each morning, spend eight to ten minutes on a rowing machine, and play racquetball three mornings a week. I have more energy, endurance, alertness, and quickness than I had 10, 15, or even 25 years ago. Exercise does make a difference in your physical, emotional, and spiritual well-being.

9

Specific Actions

What can a person do to overcome depression? Read and consider the following suggestions.

1. Try to keep up your daily routine. If you work outside the home, try to go to work each day. It is more beneficial for you to get up in the morning, get dressed, have breakfast, go to your place of work, and go through the motions of working than to remain home in bed with your discomforting thoughts.

2. If your work is in the home, follow the same procedure. Consider your daily chores important. You may feel, "It doesn't matter what I do." But it does.

3. Try to get out of the house, even for very short periods of time. You might go out for the paper in the morning after breakfast, for a walk around the block or to a favorite place or store.

4. If you can push yourself to do it, try to see family members and friends as much as possible, but for very short periods of time. Don't try to entertain in your home, but visit other people informally and briefly.

5. Deliberate physical activity is very impor-

tant for overcoming depression. Involvement in any kind of physical activity that you ordinarily might like is helpful. It is difficult to remain depressed when you are singing, swimming, riding a bicycle, jogging, playing tennis, and so on.

6. If it is difficult to talk to the people you live with, write a note. Explain briefly, for example, that it is of no use to you if they try to lift your spirits by kidding you, however well-intended they may be.

7. If your friends and family are the kind of persons who think that you will be strengthened by being scolded and criticized, tell them they are mistaken. You need encouragement, support, and firmness.

8. Let your partner know what you are feeling and that your performance is not as it usually is.

9. Remember that severe depressions usually end. If you accept this fact whether you feel like it or not, each day may be easier to get through.

10. In all depressions, you need a person you can trust (a family member or a friend) to whom you can complain and express feelings of anger. If you don't have one, find one—and let your feelings out!

11. If your appetite is poor and you are losing weight, try very hard to eat frequent small amounts of food.

The authors of *Control Your Depression* offer some helpful suggestions for overcoming depression. The emphasis is upon controlling your thoughts, which is what the Word of God admonishes us to do. Read Philippians 4:6-9 and 1 Peter 1:13.

1. Become aware of your specific thoughts, so that you can identify both troublesome and beneficial ones.

2. Learn to channel your thoughts into directions that you decide are most appropriate at the moment. Thoughts are especially good to work with for two reasons:

    a)   They are always with you. You can work with them anytime, anywhere.

    b)   They are pretty much under your control and no one else's. No one can directly change the way you think.

The following list of thoughts were obtained by asking depressed and nondepressed people to rate the frequency with which they had a large number of thoughts. We picked the thoughts that were rated significantly differently between depressed and nondepressed people.

SET A

_____   Life is interesting.

_____   I really feel great.

_____   This is fun.

_____   I have great hopes for the future.

_____   I have good self-control.

_____ That's interesting.
_____ A nice, relaxing evening can sure be enjoyable.
_____ I have enough time to accomplish the things I most want to do.
_____ I like people.
_____ I'm pretty lucky.
_____ That's funny (humorous).
_____ Don't want to miss that event.

_____ TOTAL SCORE FOR SET A
(highest possible is 12)

SET B

_____ I'll always be sexually frustrated.
_____ I'm confused.
_____ There is no love in the world.
_____ I am wasting my life.
_____ I'm scared.
_____ Nobody loves me.
_____ I'll end up living all alone.
_____ People don't consider friendship important anymore.
_____ I don't have any patience.
_____ What's the use.
_____ That was a dumb thing for me to do.
_____ I'll probably have to be placed in a mental institution someday.
_____ Anybody who thinks I'm nice doesn't know the real me.

_____ Existence has no meaning, or life has no meaning.

_____ I'm ugly.

_____ I can't express my feelings.

_____ I'll never find what I really want.

_____ I'm not capable of loving.

_____ I'm worthless.

_____ It's all my fault.

_____ Why do so many bad things happen to me?

_____ I can't think of anything that would be fun.

_____ I don't have what it takes.

_____ Bringing kids into the world is cruel because life isn't worth living.

_____ I'll never get over this depression.

_____ Things are so messed up that doing anything about them is futile.

_____ I don't have enough willpower.

_____ Why even bother getting up?

_____ I wish I were dead.

_____ I wonder if they're talking about me.

_____ Things will just get worse and worse.

_____ I have a bad temper.

_____ No matter how hard I try people aren't satisfied.

_____ I'll never make good friends.

_____ I don't dare imagine what my life will be like in ten years.

_____ There's something wrong with me.

_____ I'm selfish.

_____ My memory is lousy.
_____ I'm not as good as so-and-so.
_____ I get my feelings hurt easily.

_____ TOTAL SUM FOR SET B
(highest possible is 41)

Now Summarize Your Results as Follows:
POSITIVE THOUGHTS
(Set A total):   _____
NEGATIVE THOUGHTS
(Set B total):   _____
Ratio of Positive to Negative Thoughts
(Set A total minus Set B total):   _____

To begin working with your thoughts, you need to learn to identify them. A fairly easy way to do this is to keep track of "positive" and "negative" thoughts. Positive thoughts are those that have a positive effect on your mood and reflect the good points of whatever they refer to. For example, they may reflect your good characteristics ("I am intelligent," "I am dependable," "I know how to enjoy myself"). Or they may reflect the good parts of your life ("My family is great," "My work is satisfying," "Our health is good"). Negative thoughts are those that have a negative effect on your mood, usually because they focus on bad points ("I am worthless," "I can't do anything right," "My wife is a nag," "My husband is lazy").

DIRECTIONS:

1. Using a 3x5 card, label one side of the card with a plus sign (" + " for positive thoughts) and the other side with a minus sign ("-" for negative thoughts). Use one card per day, and date it.

2. Jot down positive and negative thoughts on the appropriate side of the card as soon after they occur as possible. (If you have trouble remembering to do this, make it a habit to take a few minutes before breakfast, lunch, dinner, and bedtime to jot down the important positive and negative thoughts of the last few hours.) Sample cards are shown below.

+   Date: _____

I really feel great.
That's interesting.
I have great hopes for the future.
I like people.
A relaxing evening can sure be
enjoyable.

-      Date: _____

I'm worthless.
Can't think of anything that
    would be fun.
I'm not capable of loving.
I'll never get over this depression.
Nobody loves me.

You won't be able to write down every thought you have, of course. If you can note ten positive thoughts and ten negative ones each day, you'll be doing well. By the end of a week you will have a good sample of positive and negative thoughts. You may find that some thoughts occur to you repeatedly, that some are more disturbing than others, and, in general, that some seem to be particularly powerful in influencing your mood.

Make a personalized "Inventory of Thoughts" (see next page), including the most important thoughts you have found during your week's self-observation. Place a star next to those thoughts which are particularly helpful to you in regard to your mood. Add more thoughts to your list if you remember important ones not already included. You may want to look at Set A and Set B earlier in this chapter for ideas.

Controlling Negative Thoughts

When you are depressed, you tend to engage in a higher number of negative thoughts than when you are not depressed. These thoughts, which may have been originally caused by feelings of depression, in turn produce more depressed feelings, thus starting a destructive downward spiral. By breaking up this process, you can reduce feelings of depression and get yourself back into a more pleasant state of mind.

The following techniques have been found helpful in controlling negative thoughts. Choose one of the techniques and try it for one week,

Inventory of Thoughts

Negative	Positive

keeping a tally of the number of negative thoughts you have each day. If at the end of the week your average is less than your baseline average, the technique is working. If not, you should switch to another technique and test it for one week. Do not give up on a technique without giving it a reasonable time to work for you.

Immediately upon noticing that you are producing a negative thought, interrupt it and go back to whatever nonnegative thoughts you were having. To interrupt the thought, instruct yourself as follows: "I am going to stop thinking about that now." Then, without getting upset, let your attention flow back into nonnegative ideas. This is probably the easiest interruption method, and the one that the authors of *Control Your Depression* recommend most highly.

There are two other methods that have been found useful by some people. One method involves a stronger interruption. You should begin practicing this method someplace where you are not likely to be heard (for example, when you are home alone or when you are driving by yourself). When you are ready to begin, start thinking a negative thought and, as soon as you notice the thought clearly in your mind, yell the word "STOP!" as loudly as you can. You"ll notice that the negative thought will be pushed aside for a few seconds by the very force of the act of yelling. You should then go on thinking nonnegative thoughts. Repeat the actual yelling technique for about three days, then begin reducing the volume of the yell, while at the same time maintaining the force behind it. Continue this process until you can yell the word "STOP!" mentally, feeling the full force of the yell without making a sound. Now you are ready to use the technique in public.[30]

Sometimes you can keep a running account of your activities hour by hour so you can see the events in greater detail. A day-by-day graph such as the following will show the amount of improvement you have made.

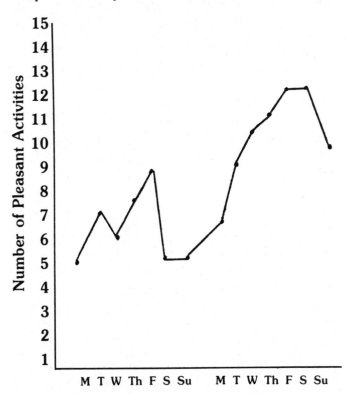

Another method that has been used successfully is to schedule activities and fix in your mind what you expect to enjoy when you engage in that activity.

ACTIVITY PLANNED _____

DATE PLANNED FOR _____

I WILL ENJOY _____

_____

I WILL ENJOY _____

_____

I WILL ENJOY _____

_____

10

Help for a Depressed Family Member

If a friend or family member is depressed, the person desperately needs someone to help him. But he or she may not be able to communicate to you what he is experiencing. If you do not feel hopeless and helpless yourself, it may not be easy for you to understand what he is going through. You may feel frustrated because of the person's inability to fully explain to you what he is experiencing. You will also be frustrated because you want to help but do not know what to do.

Picture the depressed person down in a deep pit. The pit is dark and cold and very isolated; it is frighteningly lonely. On all sides there are only rocky, muddy walls; there are no handholds or solid footholds which would provide a way to climb up and out. The person deep in the pit is totally helpless and easily becomes resigned to days of darkness and despair. There seems to be no way of escape.

This is how it feels when a person has sunk to the depths of depression. He feels overwhelmed and imprisoned by nagging but deadly feelings of worthlessness, fear, and self-blame. Concerned friends or family members stand above on the edge of the pit, yearning to help. Even so, it's very hard to call for help from the paralyzing helplessness of depression. Sometimes it's difficult to admit to others that you're even down there.[31]

As you offer help to the depressed person, pray for both understanding and patience. You will need an abundance of both. Your offer to help may be rejected at first, and it could be some time before it is accepted. You cannot just go down into the pit, grab the person, and hoist him up to the top. You would like to, but it does not work that way. The other person must be willing to trust God and other people. He must decide to begin to climb out of the pit himself. Your encouragement will be like a ladder placed inside the pit, and it may give him the motivation and hope to begin the climb.

Picture yourself at the top of the pit looking down. There is a balcony at the top, and you are leaning over the balcony cheering the person on in his climb up the ladder. Maintaining your belief in his ability to climb out may be the source of strength that he needs. When people have no hope, we need to loan them our hope until they can regain their own.

This is also a time to help the depressed person capture the hope of the Word of God as expressed in Isaiah 40:28-31:

> Do you not know? have you not heard?
> The Everlasting God, the Lord, the Creator
> of the ends of the earth
> Does not become weary or tired.
> His understanding is inscrutable.
> He gives strength to the weary,

And to him who lacks might He increases power.
Though youths grow weary and tired,
And vigorous young men stumble badly,
Yet those who wait for the Lord
Will gain new strength;
They will mount up with wings like eagles,
They will run and not get tired,
They will walk and not become weary.

If you are around a depressed person much of the time or if you live with a depressed person, you will have to protect two people—the depressed person and yourself. Why? Because the depression will affect both of you. You are dealing with someone who is very sensitive, and you must exhibit a certain sensitivity toward him. You are a giver and the other person is a receiver, but you may feel angry, hostile, and irritated at the way he is acting, which in turn will make you feel guilty for feeling that way. Because of your anger you may respond in ways you do not want to respond, and this tends to increase your anger. The depressed person will sense this and feel even worse because he feels that he is a burden on you. In time you may feel drained.

If you are depressed yourself, you should not attempt to help someone else with his depression of else you may feel overwhelmed. Your relationship could experience a strain as well.

If you have a close relationship with someone who is depressed, you will begin to notice certain symptoms at first. The first one is anahedia, which is the lack of joy in a person's life. But unfortunately, we frequently do not notice whether the person is enjoying himself or feeling pleasure. One reason is the fact that this is a very subtle change. It is an inward change that may be hard to detect. It is much easier to notice an outward change such as irritability. Irritability is another symptom of depression. Other clues are small signs of withdrawal and hopelessness.

What can you say to a friend or relative who is going through depression? Simply, "I care for you and I am available. I want to help you and be with you." Put your arm around the person and hold his or her hand. There is healing in our physical touch. A touch on the shoulder, a pat on the back, or holding the arm all convey acceptance and the feeling, "I am with you." Be honest and tell the person, "I don't understand all that you are going through, but I am trying to understand. I will be here to help you."

Part of my own commitment in my counseling profession is to pray each day for each one of my counselees. I see about 25 people a week, and I pray for them by name and for their specific situation. I share this with them and often ask what specific thing I should pray about. Many have later told me that the one thing that kept them going during their darkest hours was the fact that they knew that one person was praying for them during that time.

We may never know what our praying for and with depressed persons will do for them. In a time of depression when our friends have lost hope, we need to lend them our hope to carry them through. When they have lost faith, they need our faith to sustain them until theirs is recovered.

Most people don't know what to do for a depressed person. Here are some practical guidelines to follow. How closely you follow these will depend upon the intensity and duration of the person's depression. If he is depressed for only a few hours or a day or two, or if he is feeling down but is functioning, not all of the suggestions would apply. But if the depression has lasted for quite a while, and he is dragging around, not functioning, not eating, not sleeping, you should apply the appropriate measures.

1. Understanding the causes and symptoms of depression is the first step toward helping. If your spouse is so depressed that he just stares, ignores greetings, or turns away from you, remember that he doesn't want to act that way. In depression, the person loses the ability to govern his thinking and his emotions. If he is severely depressed he cannot control himself any more than you could walk a straight line after twirling yourself around in a tight circle 25 times. If you understand how the person is feeling and why he is acting the way he is, if you understand that his behavior is the normal behavior of a depressed person, then you can be in better control of your own responses and you will be better able to help him.

2. Watch out for suicide. The family of a depressed person should be aware of this

possibility. Any hint or statement or allusion to suicide should be talked about. It helps the depressed person to bring it out into the open and talk about it. Then he knows that other people are aware and can be called upon to help and support. Ask him to tell you about his suicidal thoughts or plans. Remember too that women make many more attempts at suicide than men, but men are more likely to succeed. A divorced man over the age of 40 is the highest risk. Any person who is so depressed that he talks about the utter hopelessness of the future might be considering suicide.

3. Get the depressed person to a doctor. Your family physician may be able to help or may recommend someone who can. The time factor is very important. Don't let depression go on and on. Even if the person keeps putting you off and refusing to go, make the arrangements, guide him firmly into the car, and go!

We can't all use this next example, but one woman found that it worked. Her husband, who ordinarily was very sociable and loved to be with other people, sat around and moped or sat in front of the TV each evening. She insisted that he see a doctor, but he refused and said that nothing was wrong. Finally she gave him an ultimatum: "You go to the doctor during the next week or I will leave! I am not going to allow you to continue in pain!" This may be a last resort, but it motivated him to seek help.

As long as you tolerate the other person's depression, you are helping to maintain it. The woman who pushed her husband to see a doctor was refusing to maintain his depression and to allow him to suffer. You may find your own creative but helpful way of encouraging your loved one to go for help.

If you are a wife with a depressed husband and you are not accustomed to taking charge, remember that your husband's illness makes it necessary to set aside your accustomed role in the marriage. Right now you are more capable of making the right decision and doing the right thing than he is.

4. Give the person your full support. The entire family ought to be made aware of the situation and given instruction as to their responses. Confrontations with the depressed person should be suspended until he achieves greater stability. Tell the family not to attack the depressed person, not to bring up his failures, not to come down hard on him, and not to ask him to do things that he is not capable of doing while he is depressed.

5. Don't avoid the depressed person. This further isolates him and could make him worse. You might avoid him because you experience guilt over his depression, thinking that you may be the cause. Remember that one person may contribute to another's problem from time to time, but no one is responsible for another person's unhappiness.

6. Understand that a depressed person really

hurts. Don't suggest that he does not really feel badly or that he is just trying to get your sympathy. Don't tell him that all he has to do is "just pray about it and read the Word more" and that will solve everything. Often a depressed person chooses portions of the Scripture that reinforce his feelings of loss and unworthiness. Any Scriptures given to a depressed person must be selected with care.

7. Empathize, rather than sympathize, with your spouse. Sympathy can only reinforce a person's feelings of hopelessness. It may make him feel more helpless and may lower his already-low self-esteem. Statements such as "It's so awful that you are depressed," or, "You must feel miserable," or, "How could this ever happen?" rarely help.

8. If your spouse is having difficulty sleeping, suggest a warm bath before going to bed; play some favorite music; or read an interesting book to him. Your involvement shows that you care. If he suffers from severe insomnia, it is helpful to sit up with him to convey to him that you care and that you are available—and also to protect against any possible suicide attempts in severe cases. Eventually he will fall asleep, and you can get some sleep then too.

If he doesn't want to eat you should say, "Look, you may not feel like eating, but you are probably hungry. Starving won't help. Food is important, so let's eat now. I'll sit down and eat with you. And then let's talk about what's troubling you." Don't harp on the food problem or on his eating habits. If you say, "Oh, you'll make me feel badly if you don't eat this food," or, "Think of all the starving people," you won't get him to eat, but you could make him feel worse. Remember, not eating is a symptom of being depressed.

9. If your spouse or other family member loses interest in activities he normally enjoys, you can gently remind him of the past enjoyment that he derived from the activities and then firmly and positively insist tht he become involved. Don't ask him if he would like to, as he might not know or may not care to respond. Don't get angry and say, "You're going with me because I'm sick and tired of you sitting around feeling sorry for yourself." You could say, "I know that you haven't felt well in the past, but I feel that you are entitled to some enjoyment. I think you might like this once we get started. And I would like to share this activity with you."

Or perhaps you call to find out what time the concert begins. Upon hanging up you say to your spouse, "I think we can get ready for it, so let's start now." If you are going shopping you could suggest, "Come along. I like to have someone with me, and you know that I do rely upon your advice." Any activity such as window-shopping, a social event, or calling a friend can be used. By getting involved, the person begins to break the destructive behavior patterns, and this helps him gain energy and motivation.

One of the best things to do is to keep the person busy. Physical activity in severe depression can be more beneficial than mental activity. His entire day might be scheduled for him. The activities planned should be those that he or she has enjoyed in the past, with all preparations made in detail.

10. If your mate begins to let his or her appearance go, don't hint about the situation. Openly, clearly, and explicitly tell him that he will enjoy fixing himself up, and perhaps will feel better for it. You could go into his room, open the shades and windows for fresh air, help him get the room in order, and lay out clean clothes.

11. Loss of confidence and self-esteem is common in depression. Don't ever kid or tease or lecture the person about his lack of confidence. And don't ignore it; it must be faced. In reactivating self-esteem, help the person see the illogic of his self-disparagement, but don't do it by berating or arguing. Look for past accomplishments in his life and get him to focus upon what he was able to accomplish prior to the onset of the depression. At this point you are trying to overcome his helplessness.

Don't join in the self-pity, but respond by saying, "Perhaps you can't do some things the way you did before, but let's talk about the things you still do well. What do you think they are?" If he says, "I can't do anything," gently name some things he can do, or draw them out of him. Be persistent and steady in your responses. Remember that at this point you have more control over your emotional responses than he has over his.

By following these principles, it is possible for us to fulfill the biblical teaching on giving empathy and encouragement to one another. Galatians 6:1 says, "Brethren, if any person is overtaken in misconduct or sin of any sort, you who are spiritual—who are responsive to and controlled by the Spirit—should set him right and restore and reinstate him, without any sense of superiority and with all gentleness, keeping an attentive eye on yourself, lest you should be tempted also" (AMP). And 1 Thessalonians 5:14 says: "And we earnestly beseech you, brethren, admonish those who are out of line—the loafers, the disorderly and the unruly; encourage the timid and fainthearted, help and give your support to the weak souls [and] be very patient with everybody—always keeping your temper" (AMP).

Study and Discussion Ideas

1. Think back over your own life and list the times that you have been depressed. Try to determine the exact cause of the depression. You may want to reread the section on causes of depression to refresh your memory.

2. If you are reading or studying this book with another person, tell him or her what helps you overcome times of depression or discouragement.

3. List ten passages from the Bible which you feel would help you the most in case you became depressed. Then select some passages that you might not want to share with depressed persons because they might misinterpret them or take them out of context.

4. Read through the first chapter of James. How would you apply James 1:2, "Consider it wholly joyful, my brethren, whenever you are enveloped in or encounter trials of any sort, to fall into various temptations" (AMP), to the problem of depression? Do you think it would help or hurt to share this passage with a depressed person?

5. Can experiences of sorrow enlarge a person's capacity for joy? How? (See John 16:20; Romans 5:3,4; 2 Corinthians 7:4; 8:2.)

6. During this next week make a graph or listing of the types of thoughts you have. Every

time you experience a positive thought jot it down and give an indication as to how you felt. Do the same for the negative thoughts. If you find that you have more negative thoughts than you want, try some of the suggestions given in this book to rid yourself of them. Keep checking to note improvement.

7. Read this book and discuss these questions together as a family. Share your reactions and develop a plan to help and encourage one another.

Recommended Reading

The Sensation of Being Somebody, by Dr. Maurice Wagner (Zondervan). This book presents some excellent biblical and psychological teachings on self-concept.

Do I Have to Be Me? by Lloyd Ahlem (Regal). Contains helpful material on adequacy and self-concept.

The Christian Use of Emotional Power, by H. Norman Wright (Revell). Presents the thought-life of a person as the basis for our emotional responses and deals with self-concept, anger, worry, and depression.

The Secret Strength of Depression, by Frederick Flach (Lippincott). One of the most helpful secular books on the subject.

Depression—Coping and Caring, by Archibald Hart (Cope Publications). One of the best Christian books written on depression.

Help for the Depressed, by Samuel Kraine (Thomas Publishers). A complete discussion of endogenous or biochemical depression.

Up from Depression, by Leonard Cammer (Pocket Books).

Notes

1. "What You Should Know About Depression," *U.S. News & World Report,* Sep. 9, 1974.
2. H. Norman Wright, *The Christian Use of Emotional Power* (Old Tappan, NJ: Fleming H. Revell, 1976), p. 76.
3. Percy Knauth, *A Session in Hell* (NY: Harper & Row, 1975).
4. Elizabeth R. Skoglund, *To Anger with Love* (NY: Harper & Row, 1977), pp. 89-91.
5. "When the Blues Really Get You Down," *Better Homes and Gardens,* Jan. 1974.
6. Richard F. Berg and Christine McCartney, *Depression and the Integrated Life* (NY: Alta House, 1981).
7. H. Norman Wright, *Making Peace with Your Past* (Old Tappan, NJ: Fleming H. Revell, 1984).
8. Frederick F. Flach, *The Secret Strength of Depression* (NY: J.B. Lippincott Company, 1974), p. 15.
9. Adapted from Wright, *Making Peace with Your Past.*
10. Archibald Hart, *Depression: Coping and Caring* (Arcadia, CA: Cope Publications, 1978), p. 11.
11. Ibid., p. 22.
12. Dr. Theodore Rubin, "Psychiatrist's Notebook," *Ladies Home Journal,* May 1976, p. 26.
13. Adapted from Wright, *Making Peace with Your Past.*
14. H. Norman Wright, *The Christian Use of Emotional Power* op. cit., p. 77.
15. Ibid., p. 78.
16. Ibid., pp. 78-80.
17. Ibid., pp. 84-85.
18. Berg and McCartney, *Depression,* p. 141.
19. David Burns, *Feeling Good—The New Mood Therapy* (NY: A Signet Book, New American Library, 1980), p. 313.

20. Ibid., pp. 319-20.
21. Adapted from Flach, *Secret Strength.*
22. Dr. Herbert Freudenberger, *Burn-Out* (NY: Bantam Books, 1980), p. 17.
23. I. David Welch, Donald Medeiros, George Tate, *Beyond Burnout* (Englewood Cliffs, NJ: Prentice Hall, 1982), pp. 13-14.
24. Elizabeth R. Skoglund, *The Whole Christian* (NY: Harper & Row, 1976), p. 12.
25. Dick Dickinson, Inter-Community Counseling Center, Long Beach, California.
26. Gary Emery, *A New Beginning* (NY: Simon & Schuster, 1981), p. 75.
27. Emery, p. 79.
28. Berg and McCartney, *Depression,* p. 117.
29. John H. Greist, Marjorie H. Klein, Roger R. Eishens, John Faris, Alan S. Gurman, and William P. Morgan, "Running as Treatment for Depression," *Comprehensive Psychiatry* 20 (1979), pp. 44-54.
30. Peter Lewisohn, Ricardo F. Munoz, Mary Ann Youngren, Antoinette M. Zeiss, *Control Your Depression* (Englewood Cliffs, NJ: Prentice Hall, 1978), adapted from pp. 175-77.
31. Berg and McCartney, p. 27.